Gong Yoga

Gong Yoga

Healing and Enlightenment
Through Sound

Mehtab Benton

Bookshelf Press

Gong Yoga: Healing and Enlightenment Through Sound
Copyright © 2013 by Michael Benton

All rights reserved. No part of this book may be used or reproduced by any means, graphic, electronic, or mechanical, including photocopying, recording, taping or by any information storage system without the written permission of the publisher except in the case of brief quotations embodied in critical articles and reviews.

Foreign publication rights available from the publisher.

Bookshelf Press books may be ordered through booksellers or by contacting:

Bookshelf Press
PO Box 50028
Austin, TX 78763
www.bookshelfpress.com
orders@bookshelfpress.com

You should not undertake any exercise or therapeutic regimen recommended in this book before consulting your personal physician. Neither the author nor the publisher shall be responsible or liable for any loss or damage allegedly arising as a consequence of your use or application of any information or suggestions contained in this book.

The author gratefully acknowledges the review of the chapter "Kundalini Yoga and the Gong" by the Kundalini Research Institute (KRI) and permission granted to include the teachings of Yogi Bhajan.

ISBN: 978-1-939239-07-5 (hbk)
ISBN: 978-1-939239-03-7(ebk)

Library of Congress Control Number: 2012956488

Contents

Preface xv
Acknowledgements.. xvii
Gong Yoga: In the Beginning..1
The Story of the Gong 3
    The Sound of the Gong 4
    The Nature of the Gong..6
        How Gongs Are Made..7
        Origin of the Gong..8
    Music and the Gong...10
        The Gong in Eastern Music 10
        The Gong in Western Music..10
The Gong and the Practice of Yoga 13
    The Gong and the Koshas...15
    The Gong and the Nadis...17
    The Gong and the Chakras...19
    Kundalini Yoga and the Gong..24
        Kundalini Yoga Mantras for Playing the Gong...........................25
        Kundalini Yoga Kriyas and Meditations....................................26
    Using the Gong in Yoga Classes..27
        The Gong and Relaxation..27
        The Gong and Mantras..27
        The Gong and Pranayama...28
        The Gong and Asanas 29
        The Gong and Kriyas 29
        The Gong and Meditation 30
        Suggestions for Using the Gong with the Practice of Yoga 30

Teaching and Practicing Gong Yoga 32
    Teaching and Playing the Gong 32
    Teaching and Practicing Without a Gong 33

Using the Gong in Healing 34
Therapeutic Applications: The Body 34
Therapeutic Applications: The Mind 36
Therapeutic Applications: The Spirit 37
Gong Yoga Therapy 38
    The Basis of Gong Yoga Therapy 38
    The Structure of a Gong Yoga Therapy Session 38
        Check-in and Evaluation 39
        Setting Intentions and Expectations 39
        Preparing to Listen to the Gong 39
        Opening the Sacred Space 40
        Creating a Map for the Journey 40
        Moving into the Breath 40
        Preparing the Physical Body 41
        Working with Breath and Sound 41
        Relaxation and Meditation 42
        Yoga Nidra 42
        The Sound of the Gong 44
        Closing the Session 44
        Re-Mapping and Integration 44

How to Play the Gong: Basic Playing Techniques 45
Getting Started 46
    Approaching the Gong 46
    Playing Position 46
    Holding the Mallet 47
    Priming the Gong 47
Striking the Gong 48
    PRACTICE SESSION #1: The Mallet Stroke 50
        Practice: The Up Stroke 50

- Practice: The Down Stroke 50
- Practice: Alternating Strokes 50
- Practice: Stilling the Gong 50
- Practice: Striking on approach 50
- Practice: Striking on departure 51
- Practice: Stabilizing the gong 51

The Playing Areas of the Gong 52
- Practice Session #2: Exploring the Areas of the Gong 54
  - Practice: Exploring the Center, Mid-Area and Rim 54
  - Practice: Finding the Sweet Spot 54
  - Percussion Points 55
- Practice Session #3: Playing the Percussion Points 59
  - Practice: Up Stroke Points 59
  - Practice: Down Stroke Points 59
  - Practice: Center Points 59
  - Designating a Sequence of Strokes 59

Creating a Sound Sequence 61
- Practice Session #4: Playing Sequences 61
  - Practice: Playing Around the Face 61
  - Practice: Playing the Diagonal Points 63
  - Practice: Multiple Strikes on Single Points 63
  - Practice: Putting Sequences Together 63

Loudness and Volume 64
- Practice Session #5: Controlling Volume 64
  - Practice: Controlling Volume through the Strike 64
  - Practice: Controlling Volume through Repetition 65
  - Practice: The Thunderbolt Strike 65

Rhythm Rates 67
- Practice Session #6: Working with Rhythms 67
  - Practice: Establishing Rhythm Rate 67
  - Practice: Rhythm Rate Variations with Sequences 68

Continuing Your Practice 70

How to Play the Gong: Advanced Playing Techniques 71
    Combination Strokes: Ties and Slurs..71
        Practice Session #7: Combination Stokes 72
    Pulsing The Gong and Returning the Sound 76
        Returning the Sound...76
        Practice Session #8: Creating Pulsing and Returning Sounds 77
    Gong Songs: Building Sequences into Sessions.................................78
        Beginning a Session 78
        Creating and Building Sequences..78
        Ending a Session..79
        Practice Session #9: Playing a Session of Sequences 80
        The Build and Release Cycle Sequence 81
        Practice Session #10: Build and Release Cycles 82
    Playing with Multiple Mallets and Gongs 83
        Two-Handed Playing: Executing Flams and Rolls.......................83
        Practice Session #11: Playing with Two Mallets 85
        Playing Multiple Gongs and the Gong Concert 85
    Intuitive Playing..87
        The Unstruck Sound: Anahata Nada 87
        Practice Session #12: Playing from Intuition................................89

Selection and Care of the Gong 90
    Size of the Gong..90
    Types of Gongs..91
    Mallets 92
    Gong Stands 92
    Cleaning the Gong 94
    Transporting and Handling the Gong 94

About the Author 97

Glossary..99

Resources...103

List of Illustrations

The Gong and the Practice of Yoga 13
    THE MAJOR NADIS 18
    CHAKRAS AND SOUND FREQUENCIES 20
    CHAKRAS AND GONG PLAYING AREAS 23

How to Play the Gong: Basic Playing Techniques 45
    HOW TO STRIKE THE GONG 49
    THE PLAYING AREAS OF THE GONG 53
    GONG PERCUSSION POINTS 56
    PERCUSSION POINTS AND MALLET STRIKE DIRECTION 58
    GONG PLAYING SEQUENCE 62

How to Play the Gong: Advanced Playing Techniques 71
    COMBINATION STROKE: THE TIE 73
    COMBINATION STROKE: THE SLUR 75
    COMBINATION STROKE: THE FLAM 84

Preface

Houston, Texas 1973

It is the end of my first yoga class. I am lying on the floor of a former hippie communal house freshly transformed into a Kundalini Yoga ashram. My yoga teacher looks just like the friends I drop acid with–bearded, longhaired, sparkly-eyed–except he is dressed all in white, wearing a turban and waving a gong mallet over his head.

"Just relax," he says as he sits next to the gong, "and let the sound of the gong take you where you need to go." I closed my eyes. And then God started shouting in my ears with the first strike of the mallet against the gong. A choir of orgasmic angels was riding a fire engine to enlightenment, singing a soulful wail of ecstasy as wave after wave of sound pulled me out of my body and plastered me to the ceiling, altering my consciousness faster than you can say "lysergic acid diethylamide." I had just been gonged.

All that breathing, all that movement and yoga postures, was all a preparation for that experience of union through sound, the Yoga of the Gong. My lifelong journey with yoga had now begun and my traveling companion would always be the God of Sound, disguised as a bronze metal disc.

The Gong remained a mystery to me as I plunged into the teachings and practices of yoga. I went through several teacher-training programs over the years in various disciplines and traditions, always returning to my lifelong love of Kundalini Yoga and the sound of the gong that accompanied so many classes.

I taught yoga to thousands of students and eventually began training hundreds of yoga teachers as we opened several yoga centers in Austin, Texas. There were so many resources to draw upon, sacred texts, trainings with expert yogis, and the presence of the master teacher in my life, Yogi Bhajan. I shared all these teachings with my yoga students and teachers to the best of my abilities.

Yet I always felt the lack of good foundational information and training about the gong itself. I originally purchased a gong soon after my wife and I began teaching yoga in our home, and proceeded to play it loudly and often badly as I practiced on myself and students.

To the credit of the gong itself, even a poorly played gong held a sway and a promise of what could be to students who asked for more and more of its sound. Yoga and the Gong are great teachers, and slowly I improved on my own as I figured things out.

Then one day good fortune brought me into the presence of a long-time student of Yogi Bhajan and expert Kundalini Yoga teacher, Gurucharan Singh Khalsa. He demonstrated a few playing techniques and then handed me the notes on playing the gong that were taken from a video lecture and gong demonstration by Yogi Bhajan.

I worked with those notes for a number of years and read everything I could about the gong itself. I found very little other information about a structured way that one could learn to play the gong or how to incorporate its sound into a yoga class. At the same time, my wife and I began using the gong for therapeutic work with yoga students, using it in conjunction with the techniques of Yoga Nidra, a transformational deep relaxation and guided meditation technique. I also trained the teachers in our yoga centers to play the gong as students began demanding more gong in their classes. Finally, yoga teachers from outside the Kundalini Yoga tradition, as well as therapists and counselors in other fields, wanted to learn more about this yoga and gong stuff.

From my experiences and their requests, this book was born. Like many fledgling books in a new field, I suspect it will prove initially most helpful as a pioneering effort yet hopefully be surpassed by other contributions as Gong Yoga becomes more widely known and practiced.

May you give and receive good gong.

Sat Nam.

Acknowledgements

With gratitude for the teachings of Yogi Bhajan,
Master of Kundalini Yoga and the Gong

Gong Yoga:
In the Beginning

Chanting, singing and music form the basis of all religious and spiritual practices, from the conservative fundamentalist to the hedonistic pagan, everyone uses sound to connect to their god. In the beginning was the Word and the Word was God.

So it is no surprise that Yoga, the foundation for all spiritual practices and the source of all religions, is essentially a practice rooted in the technology of sound. Indeed, the first yoga practices described in the ancient texts are not about postures, breathing, or even meditation but mantra and sound.

This relationship between sound and consciousness is the basis for all practices of yoga. All authentic yoga practices begin and end with sound. It is through sound that the transformation of consciousness occurs that is the purpose of yoga.

So regardless of the type of yoga we practice or the path we follow, we are all ultimately sonic yogis, transforming ourselves through vibrations and sound so that our frequency and consciousness align with the primal sound current that creates all spirit and nature, energy and matter, soul and body.

The yogis experienced this sound current that threads through the entire universe while in deep meditation. Akin to the flow of a cosmic river, they called this sound experience Nada. Literally meaning, "rushing," Nada was like the stream that carried the finite self into the ocean of the great Self, merging into the union of consciousness and ending in the soundlessness of Samadhi.

Although all yoga is essentially based on sound, the practice of Gong Yoga explicitly uses the musical sound of the gong to create an extended state of spontaneous meditation and therapeutic relaxation that facilitates the movement of prana (vital life energy) through the body for healing and awakens the consciousness for transformation.

The use of the gong in yoga and meditation can be linked back in time to Northern India where it was played by Kundalini Yoga masters to awaken the intuitive faculties and create a transcendent state of being. While the gong is still intimately associated with Kundalini Yoga in the west, it is essentially the instrument of Nada Yoga, the yoga of sound that underlies all yoga practices and traditions. The Gong is truly the instrument of the Yogi.

The practice of Gong Yoga begins with sequences of asanas, mudras, bandhas, paranayams, and mantras to open the flow of energy and to create a receptive body-mind state for guided deep relaxation and meditation. While in the relaxed and meditative state, the gong is played to cleanse the subconscious and awaken the practitioner to a transcendent state of awareness. It is a perfect union of consciousness and sound.

So why the Gong? Why not another musical instrument? What is it about the Gong that makes it so especially effective in the practice of yoga? What is its story and what can it offer us as students and teachers of yoga?

The Story of the Gong

The gong has been involved in every kind of human activity, from the earthly to the ethereal. In Buddhist monasteries, gongs call the attention of the gods. In ancient Greece, they open the realm of the dead. In Borneo, they are beaten to frighten away storms. In Ceram, gongs are given as wedding gifts. In Assam, they are used as funeral pyres. During war, gongs intimidate enemies and gather troops. In peace, they celebrate festivals and accompany dances.

Gongs are considered magical by many civilizations. They are used to heal the sick, banish evil spirits, and summon the elements. Even the touch of gong was said to rid the body of disease and give happiness and strength. Gongs were a sign of prosperity and used as currency. Princes and chiefs demonstrated their wealth and announced their rank by the gong they owned. Oaths were enforced by drinking from a gong. Southeast Asians believe each gong has a soul, and they give them names of respect, such as "Venerable Tiger" or "Sir Earthquake."

The gong has played an important role in ceremonies, rituals, and inner journeys among all the world's peoples. Deaths, births, marriages, and initiations were all accompanied by the sounding of the gong. More than simply a musical instrument, the gong is an agent of transformation. When the gong is played, the body, mind, and spirit change.

For thousands of years, across all civilizations, all who hear it instinctively recognize the power of the gong. So powerful is its sound, the gong became an object of worship to some people, a portal to God for others, and for everyone a presence that demands undivided attention.

Where does its power come from? How is it different from other musical instruments? The answers lie within the sound of the gong itself.

The Sound of the Gong

When we hear the gong for the first time, it challenges us to experience sound in a surprising and almost totally unique way. It is unlike any other musical instrument, both in how it behaves and how it interacts with the listener.

All musical instruments produce a sound envelope when played. The sound envelope consists of the initial sound made by the instrument when it is set into play, such as plucking a guitar string or striking a piano key, and then the accompanying decline of its sound over time. Most musical sounds have a predictable decline of sound (called the "decay") after the initial play or moment of impact (called the "attack.") The attack and decay cycle of an instrument's sound envelope determine how the listener experiences the sound.

For example, the sound envelope of wooden blocks, one of the earliest primitive musical instruments, begins with a sharp attack as the blocks are clapped together and declines quickly as the sound dissipates almost immediately producing a characteristic brittle sound. The sound envelope of wind instruments begins with a soft attack as the breath is blown into the instrument and ends with a gradual decay as the breath of the performer fades away. Both types of instruments produce a sound decay that is linear and predictable to the ear.

The sound envelope of a gong, however, is unpredictable, non-linear and indeed trans-spatial. After the strike by the head of the mallet, the gong's sound swells to an initial peak and begins to decay smoothly. After the first decay, however, the gong's sound returns of its own accord without any additional attack and builds to a second and even higher sound peak before finally fading away. The gong's sound envelope is like the delayed action of a wave that falls and then returns to an even higher level. This wave-like movement of peaks and valleys in the gong's sound carries the listener farther and farther on a journey, much like the swelling tides of the ocean, always returning and building again and again.

This returning sound of the gong was once described by Yogi Bhajan, the master of Kundalini Yoga and the Gong, as "resound." He explained that the "gong is not the sound, gong is the resound. Before resound you have no power. You go in the mountain, you say one word, that echo will go thousands times more, thousands of miles. That is the power of the resounding sound or anahad (note: sound without limit or boundaries). Unlimited sound vibrates and creates light and creates life."

Because of its returning sound or "resounding," the gong produces a complex synthesis of blended overtones that allow the listener to learn to listen in a completely new way. As the returning waves build on each other to produce new and intricate tones, the sound of the gong becomes so complex, so unpredictably translinear, the human mind is unable to categorize it.

As a result of the mind's inability to identify and predict the sound, people often hear a multitude of other instruments within the sound of the gong as the mind creatively attempts to compare and contrast what this sound could be. With eyes closed, some people are convinced that other music or instruments or electric amplification must be used to create the complexity and texture of the sound made by a single gong. Even with eyes open, people hear bells, drums, harps, horns or even voices singing as the gong is played.

This entirely personal perception of the gong's sound is due to its undertones. These undertones, which are produced when loud tones are sounded together, are known as combination tones. Acousticians consider combination tones to be a physiological phenomenon, rather than an acoustical one, because the tones are actually synthesized within the inner ear of each listener by the vibration of the cochlea, or extremely delicate hairs. The gong thus produces an inner sound as well as an outer sound. It is this dual sound that takes each listener deeper into their own experience of being so that the sound of the gong becomes individually unique to each person.

Dane Rudhyar in his book The Magic of Tone and the Art of Music refers to this inner sound of the gong as a "holistic" resonance in which the non-harmonic and non-periodic tones lead the listener into the non-ordinary realm of the spirit. "Perhaps more deeply than anything else," Rudhyar writes, "gongs are the concrete, physical manifestations of the sounds of the souls of the great universal religions."

The only comparable musical sound to the gong is made by large church bells whose peals produce similar complex combination tones that also take the listener out of ordinary reality. It is interesting that both the church bell in the West and the gong in the East have both been associated with the ability to call and remind its listeners of an otherworldly plane of experience.

Because the sound of the gong is so uniquely individual in the combination tones produced at the moment of playing, it is difficult to capture its sound with a recording. Many people describe a recorded gong sound as somewhat flattened, and its most powerful effects are experienced when the gong is played live within the immediate presence of the listeners.

The Nature of the Gong

The gong belongs to the musical family of instruments known as idiophones, or "self-sounders." Idiophones make a sound when scrapped, rubbed, or hit without the intervention of other materials. The sounding substance (the body of the gong in this case) is its own source of vibration, receiving acoustic energy and transmitting it in the same action. The other musical instrument families, such as aerophones (horns and woodwinds), membranophones (drums), and chordophones (stringed instruments), are "coupled sound-producers" and require the resonant support of a structure (such as the body of a guitar or air column of a flute) for the vibrations to produce the music. The gong, as well as wooden temple blocks and bells, are ancient idiophones. Modern idiophones include the xylophone, cymbals, and castanets.

Gongs are usually circular (although a polygonal form is encountered in Borneo and a triangular form exists in India), often have turned rims, and are made of metal. Traditionally, gongs are made of bronze, although other metals and alloys occur, such as bell-metal in India, beaten iron in Africa, gold in China, and silver in Tibet (the addition of silver produces a farther reaching sound). Typically, gongs are composed of 70% to 80% copper and 30% to 20% tin with the addition of lead, nickel, iron, or zinc. Instruments of lesser quality generally have a higher proportion of tin (or lead) to copper.

The surface of a gong is either flat or has a central raised dome, or "boss," in the middle. Flat gongs have an indefinite pitch and are known in East Asia as male gongs. The oldest known form of gong appears to have been flat. Bossed gongs (with a raised center) have a definite pitch and are known as female gongs. Bossed gongs, and those with a deep rim, are invariably struck in the center from where the tone issues. Flat gongs are struck off-center. The tone of the bossed gong does not differ from that of the flat gong but is definite in pitch. The gongs of China are both bossed and flat; those of the Southeast Asia islands and Africa are bossed, and those of India are flat. Gongs produced for Western music are both bossed and flat.

Gongs are also differentiated into two other categories: those that are suspended vertically and those that are horizontally placed. Single gongs are usually suspended vertically. Horizontal gongs are often placed together in groups on two crossed or parallel strings within a wooden frame and are in greatest use in Southeast Asia.

Gongs come in a wide variety of sizes, from those under six inches in diameter and carried by hand to those nearly nine feet in height. The average size of most gongs used in Western music range from 24 to 40 inches in diameter. Gongs are usually sounded with a beater or mallet, although in Java the player's fist is also used.

How Gongs Are Made

The art of gong making has always been hidden in myths and mystery. The original gong makers often fasted, prayed, and performed other austerities before beginning their craft to enlist the higher powers. Javanese gong smiths assumed a secret identity and assumed to protect themselves from malicious entities. On the day the gong was made, the gong smith meditated and chanted mantras as the art of gong making was considered to be a sacred practice.

Traditionally, the four principal centers for manufacturing gongs were China, Burma, Annam, and Java. Gong making later spread to the West in the late 19th century with the Italians, and then to Germany and Switzerland.

The traditional gong manufacturing process consisted of heating, pouring, hammering, smoothing, tuning, and polishing. The base metal copper is first melted and then the other metals added and stirred together. When ready, the molten metal is poured into a wax or clay molds or cakes of metal that are then shaped by constant hammering as the metals cool. With a large gong, the heating and hammering process might occur over a hundred times. When fully shaped, the gong is plunged into cold water to keep the metal elastic as it is tuned. After the gong is completely cooled, the gong smith begins an extensive tuning process by hammering the striking positions of the gong on both the inside and the outside. The sound is tested and then re-hammered to refine. For high quality gongs, three separate tuning processes may be necessary to produce the desired sound. Often the tone improves with age over 20 to 30 years. Finally the tuned gong is polished and ornamented.

In the West, gong making in the 21st century (such as done by the European firm of Paiste) differs from the traditional Asiatic method of pouring molten metal into molds. In this case, the gongs are cut from tempered rolled sheet metal into circular discs that are then heated and shaped by individual hammer strokes. After the gong goes through reheating and hammering, the instrument rests for three to four months before it is tuned and polished. Each gong becomes an individual work of created art with its own distinctive personality and some say sound.

A finished gong is noted primarily by its circumference size in inches or centimeters and by the frequency or tuning of sound. It is also distinguished by the number of distinctive sound waves it makes when struck. High-quality gongs usually produce twelve or more of these distinctive returning sound waves when individually struck.

Origin of the Gong

The gong is an ancient instrument of unknown origin. The gong is first mentioned at the beginning of the sixth century in China where it first appeared in Hsi Yu, a region located between Tibet and Burma. The gong, however, was not originally a Chinese instrument. The Chinese ascribed the gong's origin to another culture farther west, which some historians believe to be in northwest India, or the area now known as Afghanistan, where it was probably used in Buddhist rituals.

Some ethnomusicologists speculate the gong may have come from Greece and then spread to northwest India with the expedition of Alexander the Great. There is reference to gong-like instruments in Grecian culture as early as the eighth-century B.C. Plutarch writes about the bronze "drums" the Parthian troops used to intimidate their enemies. The Greek instrument called the echeion, used in plays to produce thunder of the gods and to signal the climax of a rituals, may actually have been an early form of the gong. The Greeks also used the echeion in death rituals in Eleusis and Sparta, much like other cultures have used the gong in funeral rites. Most likely, however, the origin of the gong predates even Aegean civilization.

The gong may have appeared as early as the Bronze Age (circa 3000 BC to 2000 BC) when tools and weapons were first made from bronze. The first gong may have been a bronze shield that was struck in war to signal an attack or retreat. Another possibility is that the first gong evolved from a bronze disk made to represent the sun that was worshiped by early farming cultures. In any case, it is probably safe to assume that the gong has several origin points in history and locales since there are many different types found all over the world.

In the West, Romans used gongs and metal disks (discus) as signal instruments. A rimmed gong from the first or second century A.D. Roman Empire was discovered in Wiltshire, England. In the bible Paul mentions the "sounding gong or tinkling cymbal" (I Corinthians xiii. 1) and in fifteenth century Europe, medieval drawings depict a tormentor mocking Christ with a gong.

The word "gong" was first used in sixteenth century Europe. The word comes from the Indonesian name for the native gong instrument called "bonang," or "bonang-bonang" for the plural. Dutch colonists in Indonesia translated "bonang-bonang" as "gom-gom" which became phonetically rendered as "gong-gong" and later shortened to "gong." Interestingly enough, the Indonesian word sometimes used to describe the gong is "cakram," derived from the Sanskrit work for "chakra," or wheel which is also the designation used by yogis for the esoteric energy centers of the subtle body.

Although European writers described the gong in the 1600s, it did not become a part of Western music until around the French Revolution. The gong, however, has played an important part in world music for at least a thousand years. All Asian cultures use the gong, and each country's gong has its unique characteristics. For example, Indian gongs are usually small with a flat surface and give a high pitch. Burmese gongs are much thicker than their Chinese counterparts. In Java, sets of tuned gongs are played together. Elsewhere around the world, gongs are made for a variety of musical and ceremonial uses. In Africa, large suspended gongs made of iron are used in the Ethiopian Coptic church. In South America, gongs discovered in Peruvian tombs are slightly concave-convex and make a clear resonant sound when struck.

Music and the Gong

The Gong in Eastern Music

The first use of the gong in formal music probably occurred in China. As early as the 8th century, the gong appears in the opera The Little Shepherd. In Beijing opera, an ensemble of gongs, cymbals, and drums are used for battle scenes and for military entrances. Interestingly, in the opera of the Sichuan and Hunan provinces, gongs and drums are the only musical instruments used.

In Japan courtly music, gagaku ensembles use a small hanging gong with other percussion instruments in a time-marking fashion. The gong is also used to provide offstage music in kabuki play productions. In Japanese festival music, one musician in the five-performer ensemble plays a small brass gong called the kane.

In Korea small gongs are used in ceremonies conducted by a female shaman while people in the Philippines use gongs in their rural dances. In other Southeast Asian countries, gongs make up an important part of percussion ensembles. In Burma and Thailand, there are percussion ensembles that use circles of knobbed gongs.

The most prevalent use of gongs in musical compositions, in both the East and the West, occurs on the Indonesian islands of Sumatra, Java, Bali, and Madura. Orchestras or ensembles known as gamelans use vertically suspended gongs as well as horizontal racks of gongs with chimes, metalophones, drums, wood xylophones, zithers, and flutes to produce music for ceremonies, plays, dances, weddings, cremations, and nearly every human activity.

The Gong in Western Music

The first use of the gong in Western orchestras dates from 1791 when Gossec included a Chinese flat gong in his Funeral Music for Mirabeau. The gong was used again by Cherubini in his Requirem and by Steibelt in his Romeo and Juliet (1793) to create a somber tone. The gong was often used by other early Western composers to give an impression of sadness or gloom, as in Tschaikovsky's Symphony No. 6 (Movement IV) and Richard Strauss' Death and Transfiguration, or to heighten a climax, such as in the Overture Francesca da Rimini by Tschiakowsky.

The gong was also used by European composers to create a dramatic, exotic or even terrifying mood, such as the mysterious sounding gong in Mussorgsky's Boris Godunov or the "oriental" sounding gong in Puccini's Madame Butterfly and Griffes' The Pleasure Dome of Kubla Khan.

For the most part, the gong in Western music is used only for accent. Composer Holst in The Planets (Mars), however, does prescribe a tremolo to be played on the gong throughout 39 bars. Stravinsky used two gong players for his Introitus (1965), while Straus wrote for a tremolo on four gongs for Die Frau ohne Schatten (1919) and Puccini scored for a series of Chinese gongs in his Turandot.

The gong is also a choice for modern Western composers who strive for unusual sounds. Stravinsky, for example, requested a rapid glissando be played on the surface of the gong with a triangle beater for his Rite of Spring ("The Sacrifice"). Penderecki had the gong vibrated with a bow for his Dimensions of Time and Silence (1960), and in John Cage's Double Music (1941), the gong was struck and immediately lowered into a tub of water to flatten its pitch.

Not all uses of the gong in the West are restricted to formally composed music. In Eastern Europe around the seventeenth century, Macedonian monasteries used a thick gong suspended in the middle of the monastery to call the monks to services. In some Catholic orders, the gong was used much like the bell to summon worshippers. During the nineteenth century among the European upper class, the gong was used to summon servants or gather the family for meals, as well as to announce the arrival of guests on formal occasions.

The gong found new popularity in the psychedelic music of 1960s and 1970s as its head-tripping sounds reverberated in the minds of the freshly stoned. The Moody Blues open their album "Days of Future Passed" with a rolling gong crescendo and close their performance with a commanding single stroke that fades into silence. Led Zeppelin uses the sound of the gong in their song "What Is And Never Should Be" and John Bonham of the group plays a 38" Paiste Symphonic gong in their song "Moby Dick." The group Aerosmith used the gong in their song "Dream On" and Queen's classic "Bohemian Rhapsody" ends with the sound of a massive gong played by Roger Taylor. Doane Perry of Jethro Tull played a 36" gong in his performances. And in the Pink Floyd concerts from 1967 to 1973, Roger Waters brought the gong on stage for "A Saucer Full of Secrets" and "Set Your Controls for the Heart of the Sun" which ended with the gong itself bursting into flames, just in case the local acidheads were not yet fully blown away.

The discovery and use of the gong by the drug culture musicians of the twentieth century was the first instance of the gong being used in Western music as a tool for conscious transformation, a harkening back to its Eastern roots of centuries past where it was also played to awaken the higher centers of the meditative mind.

Although the gong has been used as an instrument in many types of world music, its most profound use lies within its singular ability to transform, heal, and elevate the spiritual seeker and seer. Today the gong has found a new audience among therapists, yoga teachers, and individuals who seek to transform themselves and others through the power of its sound.

There is a marked difference in using the gong as a musical instrument and as a therapeutic or yogic instrument in how it is played. While formal musical training is needed to play the gong in both Eastern and Western music, learning how to play the gong for healing and transformation requires a different set of skills, as we will discover.

The Gong and the Practice of Yoga

The association of the sound of the gong and the practice of yoga is mentioned as early as the 14th century by Yogi Swatmarama in the Hatha Yoga Pradipika, one of the seminal works on the practice of hatha yoga.

In the final chapter of the Pradipika there is a discussion of the stages the yogi passes through on his journey to enlightenment. One of the distinguishing landmarks is the experience of "hearing" the internal sounds produced by the process of the awakening of the Kundalini energy of awareness. These inner sounds progress in subtlety as awareness increases. The first stages of sound are "heard" as the sound of the ocean itself. From this roaring wave-like sound, the yogi then hears the sound of various drums that are then refined into "the sound of the conch, the gong, and the horn." Indeed, another ancient text notes that when the Kundalini energy awakens the heart center, the listener experiences an internal silent sound like "a gong exploding at the center of the sun." Gradually the crashing sound of the gong dissolves until the yogi hears only a humming like that of the honeybee and becomes completely absorbed.

This state of absorption in sound until all else dissolves save the bliss of experience is also known as Laya Yoga. As the listener becomes fully involved with and completely absorbed by the external sound of the gong, the distinction between the listener ("self") and the sound ("not self") dissolves into a union, much like what occurs during the practice of Laya Yoga. The ability of the gong to create an external sound so uniquely individual to each listener that the mind becomes entranced and stilled make it a powerful instrument for inducing a meditative state.

As the sound waves of the gong suspend the thought waves of the mind, the listener is brought to a zero point, the yogic state of shunya, an original state of sweet nothingness and the first stage of Nada Yoga. The ability of the gong to quiet the mind, to halt it in its tracks, and to overcome its hold upon the consciousness was well expressed by the master Kundalini Yoga teacher Yogi Bhajan who once said, "To the mind, the sound of the gong is like a mother and father that gave it birth. The mind has no power to resist a gong that is well played." According to Yogi Bhajan, the mind must surrender to the sound of the gong within 3 to 90 seconds of being played.

With the surrender of the lower mind to the sound of the gong, the listener enters into the transcendental state of shunya or nothingness, where inner truth can be accessed and visions spontaneously arise. In this respect, the gong is the yogi's instrument for creating a spontaneous meditative state that only requires the listener to let go and let gong.

The Gong and the Koshas

The five yogic koshas, or sheaths of existence, are an important concept in understanding how yoga works and the role of the gong in effecting transformation.

Think of the self as having five wrappers or layers. The outer wrapper is the physical body (anamaya kosha), the second layer is the energetic or breath body (pranamaya kosha), the third layer is the emotional body (manamaya kosha), the fourth layer is the knowledge body (vijnanamaya kosha), and the final fifth layer at our core and essence is the bliss body (anandamaya kosha).

Through the practice of yoga, from the gross to the subtle, all five koshas of the self are affected. Practicing asanas, or yoga postures, strengthen the physical body (anamaya kosha) while the practice of pranayama or breath control works on the pranic body (pranamaya kosha). The emotional body (manamaya kosha) that processes our mundane thoughts and feelings is accessed through mantra and sacred sound. The knowledge body (vijnanamaya kosha) is essentially affected through meditation and the bliss body (anandamaya kosha) is experienced through the integration of all five sheaths.

In this kosha model, the sound of the gong affects the manamaya kosha and thereby serves as the intermediary between the physical and breath body (anamaya kosha and pranamaya kosha) and the knowledge body or meditative mind (vijnanamaya kosha). The gong helps to bridge for what is for many practitioners the great leap in a yoga practice: a movement from the grosser to the subtle regions. When mantra is used or when the gong is played, the manamaya kosha is affected, strengthened and healed much in the same way that asana does for the physical body or pranayama does for the breath body.

Because it affects the emotional sheath or body, the sound of the gong often brings about various emotional releases, especially when heard the first several times. Crying or laughing may be common, as well as experiencing transient states of anxiety, fear, love or bliss as emotional reorganization is brought about by the sound of the gong.

Gradually as the manamaya kosha interacts with this sound, the various emotional states subside and the general feeling is one of well-being. From this calm and neutral emotional center, it is then easier to experience the meditative mind of the vijnanamaya kosha.

The ability of the gong to awaken the intuitive mind and discerning intelligence (known in yoga as the buddhi mind) through its effect on the sixth chakra enhances the capacity of the listener to integrate the vijnanamaya kosha. Particularly at that moment of silence when the sound of the gong stops, the listener is given the experience of oneness in the stillness where the real is more easily distinguished from the imagined.

Finally, the gong itself can be an instrument of bliss, allowing for a merger into its all-encompassing sound that reminds the listener that the source of their existence comes from the causal center of the eternal soul, the anandamaya kosha.

One can trace the sound of the gong as it interacts with all five koshas, from the purely physical sensation of sound (anamaya kosha), to the movement of energy through the nadis (pranamaya kosha), through the synchronization of the emotional state with the mind (manamaya kosha), leading to the intuitive insight (vijnanamaya kosha) that allows for the experience of integrated bliss (anandamaya kosha).

The Gong and the Nadis

In yogic anatomy, the nadis are the rivers of energy that flow through the energetic or subtle body, much like the concept of the meridians in Eastern medicine. These energy channels carry the prana or vital life force and play a key role in the awakening of the Kundalini energy of spiritual awareness. When the gong is played, these nadis can be cleared and the listener experiences an increased flow of energy into areas that may have formerly been blocked.

This increased flow of prana through the nadis and the resulting increase in vital energy is one of the ways the gong serves as a healing instrument. In addition, the freer movement of prana through the nadis awakens, balances, and strengthens the energy of the chakra system.

One way to use the gong to work with these energy channels is to consciously breathe through alternate nostrils, a pranayama practice know as nadi shodhana, while the gong is played. The breathing practice works on the two major nadis, the ida and the pingala, as well as the two hemispheres of the brain. When coupled with the sound of the gong, this practice can bring into balance the sympathetic and parasympathetic nervous systems.

Another way to work with the gong and the nadis in the energy body is to practice listening to the gong in an upright meditative posture with the spine consciously lengthened and held steady through a gentle lock of the bandhas, or yogic muscular locks, with a very slight squeezing along the spine. The listener places the sound of the gong into the spine and tries to experience the sensation of sound in this central channel of the body that is energetically known as the sushumna nadi, or the major central nadi between the ida and the pingala. In this way, movement of energy may be facilitated through this central nadi to balance the chakras.

Occasionally the sound of the gong produces what some listeners describe as tingling sensations or movement of energy in the body. These sensations often occur as the sound of the gong clears blockages in the nadis that may have existed since birth or have resulted from traumas. On the most basic level, the gong has a balancing effect on the nadis and consequently the sympathetic nervous system (represented by the pingala nadi), the parasympathetic nervous system (the ida nadi) and the autonomic nervous system (sushumna nadi).

THE MAJOR NADIS

The major nadis (energy channels of the body) are represented by the center line (sushumna nadi), and the intersecting right line (pingala nadi) and the left line (ida nadi) that cross at each chakra.

The Gong and the Chakras

In its simplest form, a chakra is a center of energy in the subtle body that affects and controls various arenas of the human psyche. Each chakra has a unique vibration frequency that resonates with a particular physical, psychological and spiritual quality. There are seven major chakras in the classical yoga systems and each one has a specific sound quality or note that expresses its nature and identity.

For example, there is a bij mantra, or seed sound, associated with each chakra. This seed sound resonates with the energy of the chakra, expressing and ultimately balancing the chakra. These traditional sounds for the chakras are as follows:

First—LAM
Second—VAM
Third—RAM
Fourth—YAM
Fifth—HAM
Sixth—AUM
Seventh—Silence

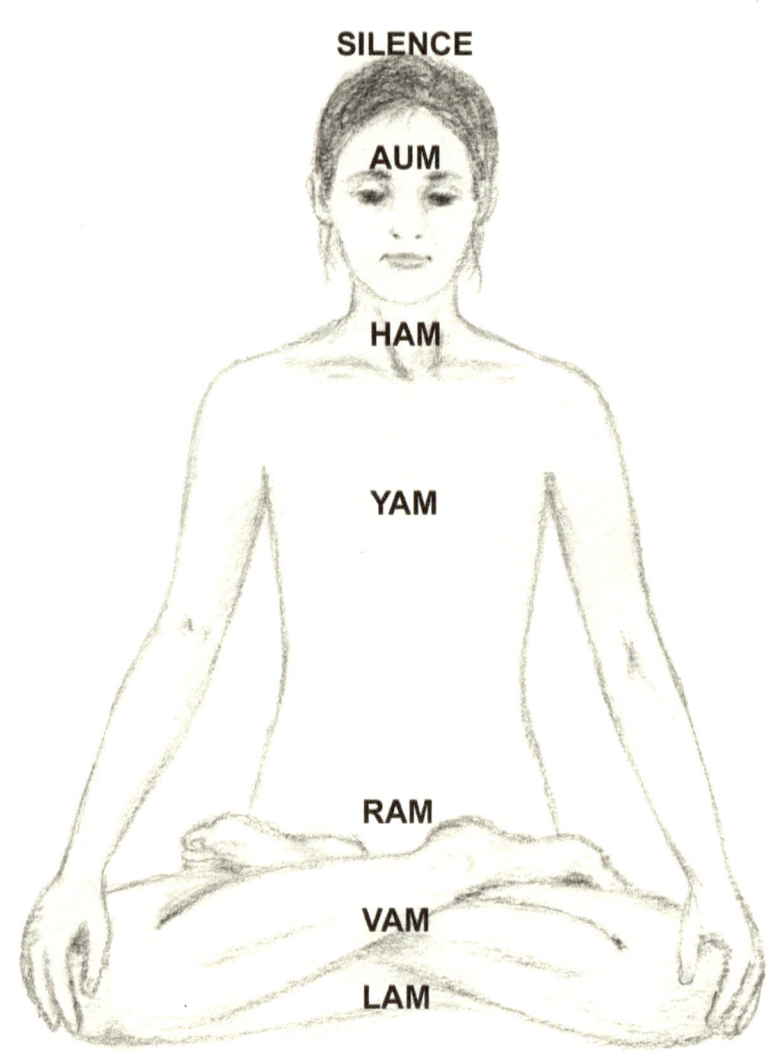

CHAKRAS AND SOUND FREQUENCIES

The bij mantras (seven sound frequencies) associated with each of the seven major chakras.

In the practice of Kundalini Yoga, various mantras also vibrate with each chakra, as in the case of the bij mantra SAT NAM for the third chakra or WAHE GURU for the sixth chakra.

In addition, there are musical notes associated with each chakra. In the Indian scale of music, these seven notes for the chakras are SA, RE, GA, MA, PA, DHA, NI, SA. The actual musical note depends upon the key; for example, in C Major the sound SA corresponds to the C note and the first chakra.

Because of this intimate relationship between sound frequencies and chakras, the gong is a powerful instrument for opening and balancing the flow of energy through them. As the gong is played with its wide range of complex frequency patterns, the chakras begin to come into a natural resonance. It is as if there were a million notes being played simultaneously until the perfect melody is struck for each specific chakra.

This collective wave of overtones and combination tones address the widest possible range of needed sounds to vibrate each chakra to its optimum resonance. In effect, there is a grand tune-up of the chakras that releases a free flow of energy that creates a sense of fluidity and responsiveness in the energy body of the listener.

Not only do all the chakras benefit from the sound of the gong, there are specific effects on individual chakras as well. This effect of the sound of the gong on a specific chakra was amply demonstrated hundreds of years ago when it was played in the courts of the kings to stimulate the sixth chakra and awaken the psychic faculties of the seers and prophets.

The royal advisers played the gong to stimulate the sixth chakra, or intuition center, where they could thereby enter a trance-like state to foretell the outcomes of battles and crop harvests. One such prediction made while listening to the gong was that the king's warriors should shoot their arrows up in the air at a particular trajectory, rather than directly at the enemy, so that the force of the falling arrows would thereby pierce the enemy's heavy armor. Similarly, the seers use the sound of the gong to awaken the intuitive faculties of the sixth chakra to foresee weather patterns that might wreck ships or create severe droughts.

Historically, the gong was also played at the time of dying in order to open the seventh, or crown, chakra at the top of the head, the traditional exit point according to yogis for the subtle body or soul to leave at the time of death. Because of this ability of the gong to open the crown chakra and allow for the easier passage of the soul, playing the gong became associated with funerals in the East and even later incorporated into Western funeral music of the 18th century.

The seventh chakra was also considered to be the gateway to divine guidance, just as the sixth chakra was considered to be the third eye of prophesy.

Small wonder that the gong itself became revered as a messenger of the gods, allowing the listener to hear unspoken voices (which in reality was simply the heightened state of the listener's meditative mind).

When the gong is played, blocked chakras may also open. This can be experienced or expressed by the listener as deep sighing (first chakra), humming (second chakra), laughter (third chakra), crying (fourth chakra), coughing (fifth chakra), internal light (third eye), or blissful connection (seventh chakra). Sometimes the response to a released chakra can be as dramatic as the woman who frequently experienced orgasms during a gong relaxation or the man who had an out of the body experience, seeing his body as he looked down from the ceiling.

Besides affecting individual energy centers in the body, the gong works on the chakras collectively by connecting through the energy relationships that exist between them. The chakras essentially have a dyadic relationship and work as a higher and lower pair of frequencies or vibrations. For example, the seventh chakra is the "higher" vibration of the first chakra, the sixth chakra is the higher frequency of the second chakra, and the fifth chakra is the upper "octave" of the third chakra. The fourth or heart chakra has an independent frequency of its own that is tied into the electromagnetic field or aura around the body.

What this paired relationship between the chakras allows is an opportunity to play them against and with each other so that a balance can be created between the two. The sound of the gong now has two counterpoints to affect. For example, the higher frequency of the sixth chakra could be "grounded" by working with the second chakra and consequently the second chakra energy could be "elevated" through working with the sixth chakra.

In effect, the complex and interactive sound of the gong creates a cross-communication between these energy centers, releasing blocks and clearing old patterns that allow the subtle body to smoothly re-integrate and the chakras to coordinate. In particular, by its coordinating and stimulating actions upon both the pituitary and pineal glands, the gong is especially effective in opening the 6th and 7th chakras and that makes it an ideal instrument for meditation.

In the accompanying illustration are the seven major chakras associated with the playing areas of the gong, beginning at the bottom of the gong, right above the rim area, for the first chakra and ending near the top of the gong, right below the rim area for the seventh chakra. The heart center, fourth chakra, is represented by both areas directly above and below the center of the gong. In Kundalini Yoga, an eight chakra is posited (generally thought of as the aura that surrounds the energy body and the seven chakra field) and this is associated with the rim area around the gong face.

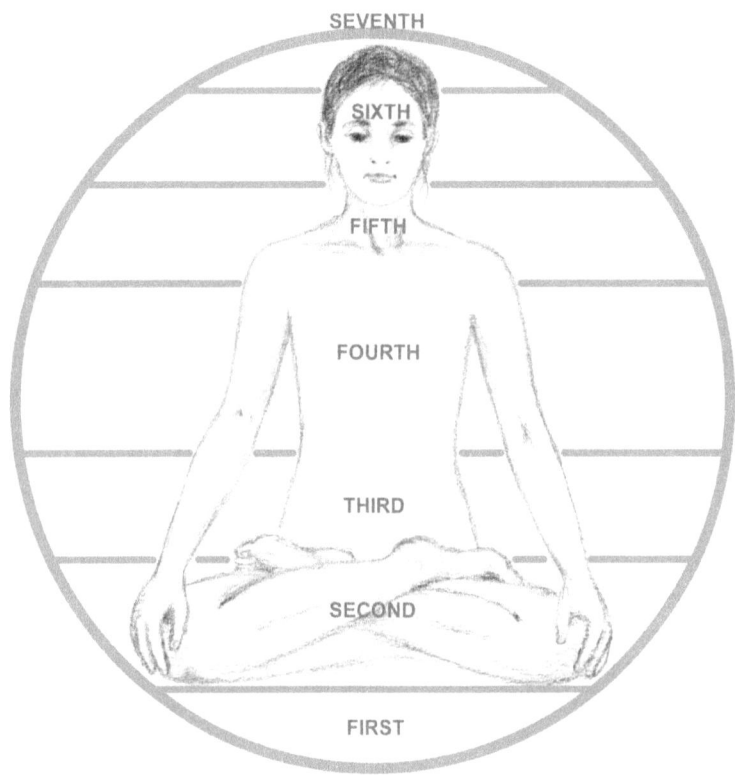

CHAKRAS AND GONG PLAYING AREAS

The middle playing areas of the gong associated each of the seven major chakras. Each horizontal lined area of the gong holds the frequencies of the corresponding numbered chakra. The eighth chakra, or aura, corresponds to the rim area of the gong.

Kundalini Yoga and the Gong

The most visible and widely employed use of the gong in yoga in the Western World is in the Kundalini Yoga tradition as taught by Yogi Bhajan. An acknowledged master of Kundalini Yoga, Tantric Yoga, and the Gong, Yogi Bhajan learned the techniques of playing the gong while still a boy from his teacher, Sant Hazara Singh, a Sikh yoga master who mentored him in the northern area of India in the 1930s and 1940s.

Bringing the teachings of Kundalini Yoga to the West in 1968, Yogi Bhajan began using the gong in his Kundalini Yoga classes in Los Angeles as early as 1969 where he played a 28-inch Paiste gong. The amazing experience with the gong in his classes inspired his students and teachers to play the gong in their classes as well. During the 1970s with drug use rampant, Yogi Bhajan directed Kundalini Yoga ashrams around the world to have a gong to play to help heal the students whose nervous systems were damaged by drugs.

His Kundalini Yoga students and teachers, past and present, have developed workshops, CDs, and trainings based upon his teachings on the gong as a sacred instrument of the yogi. More so than any person, Yogi Bhajan was the instrumental force in popularizing the use of the gong in yoga and meditation in the Western world.

The relationship between the gong and the practice of Kundalini Yoga is a natural outgrowth of the use of mantra and music as an essential part of the practice. As taught by Yogi Bhajan, Kundalini Yoga is based upon the sound current, the power of word and mantra, and the vibration of the infinite: "If you will meditate on the primal sound," he has said, "you will see the unseen, you will hear the unheard, and you will feel the unfeelable."

This primal sound is best represented by the sound of the Gong itself. "The gong is the first and last instrument for the human mind," Yogi Bhajan said. "There is only one thing that can supersede and command the human mind- the sound of the Gong. It is the first sound of the universe. It is the basic creative sound."

Generally, the gong may be played in a Kundalini Yoga class as part of a meditation or more often during relaxation at the end of class after the physical body has been prepared through a series of movements, exercises and breathing techniques known as kriyas.

Kundalini kriyas, or sequences of yoga techniques, are the most effective way to prepare the body and mind through yoga to experience the gong. For the gong yogi, a background in Kundalini Yoga is highly recommended.

Kundalini Yoga Mantras for Playing the Gong

As we will discuss later in the section on playing the gong, the gong player should first attune himself or herself to the power of the sound of the gong itself before playing it. This linkage between the player and the gong creates the intuitive relationship that allows the gong to play the player as well as the player to play the gong.

In Kundalini Yoga, the specific linkage between the gong master and the gong is made with a series of three mantras, or a centering prayer. Each mantra is repeated once silently or chanted before the gong is played.

The first mantra brings you before the timeless teacher, to lay aside your ego, and to allow the wisdom through all the ages to guide you:

Ad Gurey Nameh
(I call upon the teacher who exists at the Beginning)
Jugad Gurey Nameh
(I call upon the teacher who teaches through all times)
Sat Gurey Nameh
(I call upon the teacher who teaches from the Truth)
Siri Guru Dev A Nameh
(I call upon the unseen subtle teacher of all)

The second mantra links to the creative energy of the universe, the feminine creative power that rules music and all forms of expression, the sound of ONG, of creation itself:

Ong Namo
(I call upon the Infinite Creative Energy)
Guru Dev Namo
(I call upon the divine transcendent teacher)

The third mantra takes the mind to the point where sound exists in the eternal moment of truth, beyond polarities and indistinguishable from the sound and the producer of the sound.

Ad Such
(The truth before all beginnings)
Jugad Such
(The truth through all ages)

Haibhee Such
   (The truth at this moment)
Nanak Hosee Bhee Such
   (The truth that is ever true)

Once these mantras are used with the proper intention, the gong player plays what is needed at the present moment and not from the ego of a performer. The karma of the playing becomes dharma and elevates both the player and the listener.

Kundalini Yoga Kriyas and Meditations

Although many Kundalini Yoga kriyas, or exercise sequences, can be enhanced when the gong is played during relaxation, there are specific kriyas taught by Yogi Bhajan that specify playing the gong at different points in the kriya or meditation to complete its effect.

The following Kundalini meditation is an example of how the gong is used to deepen the effect of the practice.

During this 11-minute meditation, the gong is played for the first three minutes to give the rhythm for what is described as a "heavy breath of fire." During the last 8 minutes, a mantra is played.

Here is the gong meditation taught by Yogi Bhajan on May 13, 1989 in Hamburg, Germany as part of a lecture entitled "Define Your Own Nobility." This summary is taken verbatim from the end of the transcribed lecture. The gong is played during the first three minutes.

"In easy pose, put your arms up to a 60 degree angle in front of you, elbows locked straight, palms facing down. Have your hands in gian mudra (thumb tips touch the index fingertips with the other three fingers straight.) Close eyes, and put eyes at the tip of your nose, sitting straight. Makes the gray matter move and serum change at our command. Comments: You'll get hot and different as a result of this position. To be able to maintain it, pull your shoulders out and stretch them forward, so the lower sciatica is disconnected and then the body won't shake. This posture makes you fearless, dauntlessly clear and extremely strong.

Breath of fire in this posture, for 3 minutes. Then, maintaining posture, begin long deep breathing with the mantra Humee Hum being played for 8 minutes. (Total 11 minutes.) End: Inhale, hold and stretch tight for about 20 seconds. Then breath of fire for about 15 seconds. Repeat this 3 times total. Relax."

Using the Gong in Yoga Classes

The gong may be integrated into a yoga class or a private yoga session in several ways. The most common use of the gong in the yoga teaching environment is during relaxation. Secondly, the gong may be used to enhance or guide a meditative process. In addition, the sound of the gong can be effective when used to complement an asana, pranayama or mantra practice. It can also be used to open or close the sacred space of a class.

The Gong and Relaxation

Regardless for what purpose the gong is played, it is usually played when the listener is in a relaxed state. Indeed, to use the gong effectively in a yoga class, the listener is almost always in a receptive state of awareness or relaxation. Without this engaged awareness or relaxation, the listener may encounter the sound of the gong more as a musical than a meditative experience and experience resistance to fully integrating the sound.

The gong may be played to induce or create relaxation in several ways. A hypnotic pulsing sound as discussed in the advanced playing techniques can be effective in inducing the listener to enter relaxation. Tension may then be removed by playing a "build and release cycle" (again see advanced playing techniques). To deepen relaxation, the gong may then be played softly until the session ends with a fading sound.

The sound of the gong itself is a powerful stimulant for the parasympathetic system which becomes dominant during a deeply relaxed state, particularly when the eyes are closed. It is common to hear some people snoring during a gong relaxation even when the gong is played very loudly. While many people do enjoy a gong nap, ideally the listener remains both relaxed and aware during a gong relaxation (just like in any good yoga relaxation) so the mind and emotions achieve a clear quality.

The Gong and Mantras

Like the sound of the gong, mantras are also transformational sounds that change consciousness and promote integration. Mantras may be chanted or played along with the sound of the gong to create a synergistic effect.

One way to effectively interweave mantras with the gong is to play a recording of a mantra at a low to mid-level sound. As the mantra is playing, the gong sound builds and subsides so that the sound of the mantra fades "in and out" of the consciousness of the listener. At one point the gong may completely overwhelm the mantra. At other times, the gong becomes so quiet that it is only an underlining for the mantra. Obviously the selection of the mantra and the skill of the gong player to play off the sound are critical to its effect; otherwise, the sounds may become simply competitively irritating to the listener. A safer way may be to select an appropriate mantra to either begin or to end a gong playing session, providing a gentle introduction or familiar re-entry point for the gong session.

The gong can also be played as individuals chant mantras along with the playing (usually it is difficult for the gong player to both chant and play effectively). Again, this requires skillful practice to integrate the sound of the gong to accentuate or amplify the practice of the mantra. One way to begin is to use a light rhythmical gong stroke that creates a steady pulse line for the mantras to resonate off of. A powerful group chant of a simple "seed" or bij mantra such as AUM or ONG with the accents of the gong can create a rich wall of sound that facilitates deeper absorption into the mantra. Again, the gong player must find the "voice" of the gong to make this practice effective or it can simply just become annoying.

The Gong and Pranayama

The Gong is effective in moving prana (vital energy) through the body and can be used to enhance pranayama (breathing) practices.

One way to use the gong in a pranayama practice is as a timer to signal each stage during an inhale, retention, exhale and suspension cycle. Begin the inhale and hold the breath until the gong is struck. Then extend the exhale until the gong is struck again. Hold the breath out until the gong signals the time to begin the next inhale, and so forth.

The gong can also be played during the time of retention when the breath is held out after an exhale. At this stage of pranayama, it is often common to release deep fears (e.g., the fear of death from cessation of breath) that can be quickly cleared by the directed sound of the gong at this stage.

For those who practice Kundalini Yoga with the breath of fire (a rapid and equal inhaling and exhaling technique), a common experience is that the sustained steady rhythm of the gong enhances an effortless breath pace.

Finally, the gong can be played during any pranayama practice as long as it matches and amplifies the natural breath rhythms of the pranayama. The rhythm and tempo for a breath of fire, (or kapalbhati or bhastrika, for example), is faster than for a long and deep alternate nostril breathing practice.

When skillfully used, the gong can aid in the removal of breathing blocks and the movement of the breath.

The caveat is that the gong player must be highly attuned to integrating the playing with breath; otherwise, the sound may be confounding or even detrimental to the nervous system.

The Gong and Asanas

As with pranayama, the gong can be used as a timer when working with asanas, creating a signal to flow from posture to posture with the sounding of each gong stroke.

As a posture is held, the gong may be played appropriately to enhance the energy of the asana. For example, an extended warrior pose could be accompanied by a steady almost martial tempo that is fiery and focused. A long forward bend, on the other hand, would be enhanced by a slow, watery beat that encourages release and letting go.

If the practitioner is advanced enough to hold a posture for an extended period of time (5 to 15 minutes), the gong can be helpful in accessing blocked energy flows and moving the prana along the lines of the asana. Again, the player must be skillful and cognizant of the asana practice itself to understand what is needed from the gong. Simply playing the gong while asanas are being done is not enough to make it an appropriate yogic tool.

The Gong and Kriyas

With the practice of Kundalini Yoga that is always done in prescribed sequences known as kriyas, the gong is sometimes explicitly called for at a particular point in the practice or sometimes at the end. Indeed, a length of time to play the gong may even be specified to compete the effect of the Kundalini kriya. In these cases, the gong player is safely guided in integrating the gong into the yoga experience. In general, the gong should not be played randomly during a Kundalini kriya (although it may be done so at the end) in order to not disturb the flow of prana that the kriya is intentionally creating.

If you are practicing yoga kriyas, or prescribed sequences, from other traditions as well, the gong should be used judiciously in order to not disrupt the effects of the kriya or standardized practice.

The Gong and Meditation

Perhaps one of the most common uses of the gong in yoga, along with relaxation, is to aid in meditation. Simply listening to a gong well played while in relaxed awareness will automatically induce a meditative state. This primarily occurs as the sound of the gong activates the sixth and seventh chakras and the parasympathetic nervous system.

When using the gong for meditation, as contrasted with relaxation or guided visualization, the listener should be sitting upright in a meditative posture with the spine perpendicular to the earth. Ideally a breath awareness or pranayama exercise has preceded the meditation to heighten the sensitivity to the sound of the gong.

If no specific focus is specified for the meditation, the listener can focus at the third-eye point while the gong is played and breathe slowly and consciously. An effective mudra or hand position for a seated gong meditation is to raise both hands in front of the shoulders and pulled slightly back, palms out, and hold the two smaller fingers down with the thumb while extending the index and middle fingers straight up and touching together. This Pran Bandha mudra locks the prana in the central channel of the spine and intensifies the effect of the sound.

For most listeners, a 3 to 11 minute gong seated meditation will be suitably effective followed by an equal length of relaxation. Advanced meditators can be treated to a 31-minute seated gong meditation with the provision that they have a strong nervous system not compromised by stress, trauma, or drug use; otherwise, such similar extended times of gong playing (over 11 minutes) may be best experienced in relaxation.

One general consideration when playing the gong for meditation, as contrasted for relaxation or therapeutic healing purposes, is that the sound energy be concentrated in the higher chakra centers and an emphasis placed on pulsing the gong rather than using the stronger build and release cycles that work more strongly on the physical body and lower chakras.

The meditator can also work with "hearing" the sound in the back of the head, in the spine (central channel), or at the heart center, depending upon the nature of the meditation.

Suggestions for Using the Gong with the Practice of Yoga

The gong may be incorporated judiciously throughout a yoga class with these guidelines in mind:

- Do not give complicated verbal instructions to the students while the gong is played. While it is better to not speak at all while the gong is playing, realize you will have to project loudly if you must say something vital.
- Do not over orchestrate the class with multiple gong sessions. For most people, using the gong a few times during a class will be sufficient.
- Let students know when you are about to play the gong if they do not already expect it. The unexpected entry of the gong into a yoga class is like God walking into your bedroom.
- If some students in class have never heard the gong before, prepare them for the experience with instructions to relax into the sound and use the breath to allow the experience to be received. Perhaps even have them watch you strike the gong the first time so they can see the sound being made.
- Be cognizant that some people may react negatively to the overwhelming sound of the gong the first time they hear it, particularly if they have issues around trust, letting go, tightly held boundaries, or a history of unpleasant associations with loud or unusual sounds. Ex-war veterans or victims of violence can have unpleasant flashbacks if the sound grows intense. On the other hand, these same people can develop a healthy and appreciative relationship with the gong once it begins to clear out feelings of anxiety and old traumas.
- Be aware that whenever the gong is played in the class, it will open and change energy. People may still process emotional clearing from the gong as they continue through the rest of the class and this may color the experience of the remainder of the class.
- Bring people out of the gong space gently, with the soothing sound of your voice, a period of silence, or appropriate music or other sounds. Do not rush the transition from listening to the gong to actively doing something in the class as there is sometimes a disassociation from the physical body when listening to the gong.

Affirm the benefits of the gong as an instrument to clear and release. Give permission for tears and laughter without interrupting the class or giving undue attention to an individual's processing of the experience.

Teaching and Practicing Gong Yoga

Teaching or practicing Gong Yoga obviously requires a gong be played during the class or session, and the last half of this book goes into detail how to learn to play the gong.

There may be times, however, when there is no gong or anyone available to play the gong or when there needs to be both a teacher and a gong player in order to create a Gong Yoga class. Let's look at the practicalities of integrating the gong into teaching and practicing.

Teaching and Playing the Gong

Depending upon the structure of the class and the playing skill of the teacher, the teacher can both instruct the class as well as play the gong. This works well with relaxation and meditation when the students need little guidance from the teacher.

On the other hand, if the teacher needs to actively guide the students through an asana practice or otherwise needs to be engaged in teaching, then a second person needs to play the gong. Similarly, if the teacher is not skilled enough to play the gong, then they may work with a gong player as they teach the class.

Such an arrangement requires a good rapport between the teacher and gong player so as to strike an appropriate balance between spoken instruction and the playing of the gong. The gong should be played at a very low level, if at all, if the teacher needs to speak or interact with the students. At the same time, the teacher needs to be sensitive when it is better to remain silent and let the gong do its work.

The gong player should always be in a subservient role to the teacher, neither speaking nor instructing the students, once the class has begun. In addition the gong player needs to be tuned in to the changing needs of the class as it unfolds and be ready to quickly support the teacher. Each yoga class develops a rhythm of its own according to the students and energy in the room, and the gong player must be open to change and accommodation.

Regardless if the teacher plays the gong or is assisted by a gong player, the class needs to be carefully orchestrated to maximize the impact of the sound of the gong. There needs to be sufficient listening space as the gong is interweaved into the class experience. Realize that the gong is never simply background music. It creates a dominant undertone and audible presence that moves and changes energy from moment to moment, breath to breath.

Teaching and Practicing Without a Gong

If there is no gong or gong player, or if you wish to practice Gong Yoga by yourself, then a recording of the gong may be used. The advantage to using a recording is that you can work with an existing sound and predetermined length to construct a well-planned class or practice. The drawback is that you are locked into a non-dynamic environment that you must faithfully follow.

A gong recording is helpful when you wish to teach or practice for specific intervals of time. For example, a pranayama practice can be timed exactly with the beat of the gong for an inhale and exhale ratio cycle and thus obviate the need for counting the breath intervals. Similarly, a meditation or relaxation period can be exactly timed to a gong-playing interval without the need for a clock or timer. With a regular gong beat, even asanas or postures could be held for a specific length of time before moving into the next one, thus creating an orchestrated "gong flow" of yoga movements with the breath.

Obviously the key to the success of using a gong recording in teaching and practicing is to select one that is amenable to your needs. You can look at the Gong Resources chapter for additional information on gong recordings.

Using the Gong in Healing

The gong works on all levels to heal and transform. From the purely physical, to the emotional and spiritual, the sound of the gong can promote a positive change in the listener. In addition to yogis and yoga teachers, doctors, music therapists, psychotherapists, and researchers have used the gong as an adjunct to their healing modalities. As Yoga involves the body, mind and spirit, let's look at how the gong is used in these areas to effect healing.

Therapeutic Applications: The Body

The gong produces a strong sound wave, almost tangible to the touch, which stimulates the physical body by influencing the surface of the skin. The sonic touch of the gong can be a healing touch as its sound stimulates the body's dermatomes.

Dermatomes are surface areas of skin extending from the spine throughout the body. Through a network of nerves, these skin areas are connected to different organs in the body and with corresponding segments of the spinal cord. These skin areas can be stimulated by sound waves, much like a massage, and produce effects on corresponding organs and other areas of the body.

The gong is an effective producer of sound waves that stimulate the dermatomes when played in reasonable proximity to the listener. Particularly when the gong is 32 inches or larger in diameter and played within 6 feet of the listener, a low frequency sound wave can completely encase the body in a "sonic massage."

Educator and musician Johannes Heimrath conducted many workshops and healing sessions with the gong through the 1980s. He discovered that the sound of the gong was most helpful in connection with relieving neck pain and headaches, menstrual difficulties and cramping in the chest and upper respiratory system.

Anne Kathrin Nickel and her associate researchers published an article in Music Therapy Today (September 2003) also confirmed that the gong, and other instruments, proved helpful in treating children with migraine headaches.

The European Spine Journal revealed that the gong was helpful in accelerating the healing process of acute ankle sprains. Anecdotally, a gong player and counselor obtained relief from his sprained ankle by propping his foot directly in front of a 28-inch gong and playing it for 10–15 minutes over several days. In England, a veterinarian plays the gong for horses as part of their sprain treatments to achieve accelerated healing.

On a purely physical level, the sound of a live gong stimulates circulation while its wide range of frequencies stimulates nerve endings and may prove useful in recovering from injuries in which nerve damage has occurred.

As physical distress and illness often have an emotional and stress-related component as well, the gong affects the physical health by working in these areas as well. Finally, it appears that the sound of the gong stimulates the glandular system to a higher level of functioning. The pituitary gland seems directly affected by its sound which in turn causes the whole glandular system to become balanced.

Therapeutic Applications: The Mind

As the sound of the gong creates deep relaxation, clears the mind, and stimulates the glandular system to a higher level of functioning, it also aids in the reorganization of the emotional energy and feelings that are tied into the body structure and consequently affect the mind.

In his book Music and Healing Across Cultures (2006), musical therapist David Akombo shared his research on the use of the Gamelan Gong as a historical way that schizophrenia has been treated in the Balinese culture. The illness is often viewed as much as a spiritual as a physical illness in Southeastern Asian society and the gong holds a cultural position as both a physical and spiritual agent in effecting a cure. It is used in specifically in the psychiatric hospital to help with the patient's schizophrenia.

In 1999 a study published by the German Society for Music Therapy entitled "Music Therapy with Archaic Instruments. An Innovative Method for Treating Early Disorders," Dr. Peter Hess, neurologist and psychiatrist and director of the Day Clinic Metznerpark, Frankenthal in Germany concluded that the sound of the gong was an effective therapeutic approach for working with psychotic patients. In brief, his research revealed that the trance-like state, or altered state of consciousness, induced by hearing the gong "reveals early biographical layers of consciousness and transpersonal dimensions. The similarity of the experiences in the sound trance and in the psychotic episode gives the patients the chance to integrate them. So a healing process is initiated and the patients' sense of responsibility and independence is supported."

Dorita S. Berger in her book Music Therapy, Sensory Integration and the Autistic Child (2002), recounts that no musical instrument seem to have an effect on her four-year old autistic patient until he heard the gong. In their book Clinical Applications of Music Therapy in Psychiatry (1999), therapists Tony Wigram and Jos De Backer give both a recommendation and caveat to using the gong: "The discovery of the gong was a boom to music therapy. The application of the gong became the state of the art. However, many used the gong without any expertise and this holds a danger."

The cautionary perspective on using the gong for healing and therapy is a good one. The gong is a powerful and transformational instrument. Its sound can both heal and destroy. Indeed, it was used in ancient times as both a weapon to disorient enemies as well as an inspiring call to duty. It is akin to a high-speed dentist drill, able to clean out decay or create torturous pain. Simply striking the gong during a healing session or using it as a therapeutic addendum may not work and may harm. It is an instrument to respect and use with understanding.

Therapeutic Applications: The Spirit

Perhaps the most common symptoms of spiritual malaise today are substance abuse and addictive behavior. Many researchers and therapists have recognized this connection between abusive addictions and spiritual disconnection, including psychiatrist Dr. Ray Matthew, director of the Duke University Addictions Program. His research has shown that the same pleasure centers in the brain stimulated by drugs like marijuana are also activated by spiritual experiences. Matthew observed that the key to breaking the destructive addictive response is to first "detach yourself from the pressure and content of your mind for a minute or two and you become freer from committing compulsive, automatic actions."

The gong is a singularly effective instrument to help the listener detach from the pressure and content of the mind through an induced meditative state in order to get free of habitual patterns. The spiritual healing of the gong occurs through the connection it makes between the listener and the world beyond the body and mind. It provides that experience of a non-ordinary and elevating reality that the addict often seeks through drugs.

In one incident related to me by a San Antonio pediatrician who uses the gong with her young patients is the case where a youngster began to develop a smoking habit but no longer had the impulse to smoke in just after one gong therapy session with her.

For a number of years, the gong has been used in programs for recovering drug addicts to rebuild the nervous system and to open a spiritual connection. As early as 1973, Yogi Bhajan and his students began a program in Tucson, Arizona called Superhealth that incorporated Kundalini yoga technology, including extended gong sessions, to treat thousands of recovering drug addicts. The program was accredited by the Joint Commission on Accreditation of Healthcare Organization and received its highest commendation. In its first year of operation, it distinguished itself as being in the top 10% of all treatment programs throughout the U.S, with an astounding recovery rate of 91%.

The spiritual healing power of the gong is perhaps best understood by its ability to create a non-ordinary state of transcendent reality and a connection with a vastness beyond the finite self. In this space, even for the briefest of moments, the gong is a portal to what has always existed and what can always be.

Using the gong in healing is an emerging field with many new approaches in music therapy, psychotherapy, spiritual counseling and even chiropractic care. How the gong will eventually be integrated into these disciplines hold great possibilities. Yet there is already an ancient use of the gong for healing through the science of yoga. Working with existing yoga practices in a systematic way, we can use an approach for healing and transformation called Gong Yoga Therapy.

Gong Yoga Therapy

All yoga is ultimately therapeutic as it facilitates the healing journey into Oneness. Similarly, the sound of the well-played gong is also a therapeutic instrument for self-discovery and reintegration as it creates a space for self-absorption and union through a primal sound current. While it is important to realize that the purpose of both the practice of yoga and the playing of the gong are primarily for self-transformation and enlightenment, we can certainly allow for self-healing to be an enjoyable side benefit from the therapeutic pairings of these ancient technologies together. Gong Yoga Therapy formalizes the relationship between various yoga practices with the sound of the gong to produce specific healing results.

A gong yoga therapy session can be structured to awaken intuition, clear the past, balance the emotions, align the chakras, or even improve digestion and elimination. All healing journeys can be enhanced by gong yoga therapy. The practitioner need only skillfully construct a therapy session using the applied tools of yoga and sound to produce the desired results.

The Basis of Gong Yoga Therapy

The practice of Gong Yoga Therapy begins with traditional practices of yoga such as asanas, mudras, bandhas, paranayams, and mantras to open the flow of energy and to create a body-mind state for change and healing. While in this receptive state of awareness produced by the yoga practice, the sound of the gong is used to create an extended state of spontaneous meditation and therapeutic relaxation that facilitates the movement of prana (vital life energy) through the body for healing. In this respect, the gong is merely an instrument that magnifies and focuses the power of the yoga practice.

While Gong Therapy may exist without Yoga, it is in the union of the two that their full benefits are more easily accessed.

The Structure of a Gong Yoga Therapy Session

Gong yoga therapy may be done in individual sessions, group classes or as an extended workshop experience. While there are countless healing applications for a gong yoga therapy session and the time involved can be shortened or extended, the following structure is essentially the same for all sessions.

- **Check-in and Evaluation**

    Who is your audience? What needs and issues do they have? What is the purpose of your session with them?

    A personalized gong yoga therapy session may be structured to fulfill the needs of one individual or it may be a general session suitable for a group. In either case, you need an interview process to determine the background of your audience, their previous relationship to yoga and the gong, any limitations in the form of injuries or medications that may affect their participation, and a sense of where they are in their own personal work of healing and transformation.

- **Setting Intentions and Expectations**

    What can we expect from this practice and therapy? What are the desired outcomes? How can we best experience this therapy session?

    Healing begins with intention. Suggest or guide your audience in developing an intention for the session. Also, prepare them for the experience of doing yoga and listening to the gong. If they have never heard the gong played before, allow them to watch you create a sound. Explain how the gong and yoga work together. Give hints and instructions on how to best enjoy the session and what may come up for them as a result of this work. Be clear, affirmative and inspiring as you set the expectations for the session.

- **Preparing to Listen to the Gong**

    How can you best experience the gong? What do you need to do to listen effectively?

    The gong is best experienced in a relaxed and aware state. The easiest way for most people to enter that state is through the breath. Emphasize the value of breath awareness and using the breath during a gong session to maintain the thread of awareness and conscious relaxation. Give permission for the listener to change position as they listen to the gong. Minimize any physical discomfort and environmental distractions such as temperature fluctuations, outside noise, or unnecessary movement (better to make a bathroom visit before and not during the session). If hearing aids are worn, they should definitely be turned all the way off, not just down. The eyes may be covered. If there is acute sensitivity to sound, a blanket may be placed near or around the ears before the session begins if the person is lying down. For a long relaxation period on the back, you may require many layers of blankets, bolsters, or even an air mattress to allow the person to become comfortable on the back.

○ **Opening the Sacred Space**

After the orientation and preparation for the session, both the gong therapist and yoga teacher (which can be one and the same or two different people) need to open the sacred space for healing and yoga for themselves and their listeners.

Ideally, this is done through sound or mantra. If the style of yoga used in the therapy session has a traditional opening mantra or invocation, it should be explained and then used with the listeners. If there is no traditional mantra opening, the sound of AUM may be used (or alternatively, the more centering sound of ONG).

Depending upon the group, a prayer may also be offered with or in place of a mantra. The gong may also be softly struck once to open the space. Time is given for individuals to set or remember their intention and for the teachers to center themselves in relationship to the gong and the practice of yoga.

○ **Creating a Map for the Journey**

Although not essential, some gong yoga therapists find it helpful for participants to chart or map their current state of physical, emotional and spiritual well being before beginning the actual session. This provides both a benchmark for the participant as well as an attunement for the work that is to be done.

A useful map for some people is to have them do a guided body scan while in a relaxed state. This is done by simply directing breath and awareness to the different areas of the body and allowing the participants time to experience any sensations in those areas.

At the end of the body scan, they can express their experience by sharing with a partner or group, writing in a journal, or even using paper and crayons to draw and chart their experience.

○ **Moving into the Breath**

As much of the gong yoga therapy session involves the directed movement of prana (vital life force energy) via sound to effect healing, an early connection with the breath should be made with some simple pranayama practices at the beginning of the session.

This may be a simple breath awareness exercise, long deep breathing, or listening to or counting the breath. Alternate nostril breathing (nadi shodhana) is highly recommended as well, with or without retention or ratio depending upon the experience of the practitioners. Depending upon the energy level of the practitioners and the flow of the planned session, the breath awareness exercise may be done lying down, sitting, or standing.

- **Preparing the Physical Body**

    Depending upon the focus of the session, a planned series of postures (asanas) or yoga sets (kriyas) is now done. This is where the skilled experience of a yoga teacher comes into play in the selection and design of the exercises and movements to prepare the physical body for healing and relaxation. If the gong therapist is not a trained yoga teacher, one should be present to guide the participants through the practice.

    While almost any balanced yoga practice or kriya (a prescribed sequence of exercises) will enhance a gong yoga therapy session, ideally it will be designed to complement the theme of the session. For example, a session dealing with the emotional body may have yoga postures or kriyas that center around movements and exercises that work in the area of the hips, sacral area and second chakra. A session for dealing with anger would address the heart and liver areas while a session focusing on creativity would involve the throat or fifth chakra area as well as the navel point or third chakra. Kundalini Yoga has a multitude of therapeutically specific kriyas that can be used for a wide variety of issues and are highly recommended. If there is not a specific therapeutic focus in the physical yoga practice, then it should be a practice that moves energy through the body and releases tension so relaxation can be natural and deep. Even a simple series of Sun Salutations will be most helpful. The preparation for relaxed awareness is of paramount importance in this section as well as the release of physical tension.

    Depending upon the length of the session and the ability of the practitioners, the use of asanas and kriyas may take 20 to 90 minutes. In the Panchamaya (five kosha) therapeutic model of yoga, this part of the session works with the anamaya kosha (physical body).

- **Working with Breath and Sound**

    To build a bridge from the grosser physical realm to the more subtle experience of sound, the gong yoga therapy session should incorporate breath work with the postures or have a separate time for pranayama at the end of the posture practices.

    If the participants are experienced in breath work, then pranayama practices in which the breath is held after inhalation (retention) begins to still and quiet the mind to go deeper into the experience of sound. Be aware that certain health conditions (such as untreated high blood pressure, glaucoma, eye problems, and ear congestion) are contraindicated for breath retention. Most people, however, can safely retain the breath for up to 10 seconds. The simplest practice would be to inhale for 5 to 10 seconds, retain the breath for 10 seconds, and then exhale for 10 seconds. Breath meditations would also be beneficial at this stage as well.

Depending upon the length of the session, this dedicated breath work could take from 5 to 15 minutes. In the Panchamaya therapeutic model of yoga, this part of the session works with the pranamaya kosha (breath or energy body).

Following the breath work, or in conjunction with it, mantras or toning sounds may be used to take the practitioner into the realms of sound. Making as well as deeply listening to the sounds (mantras) attenuates the listener to the power of sound to move and change consciousness. Depending upon the practice and tradition, this could take the form of a mantra meditation, the repetition of a simple mantras like AUM or ONG or toning with sounds like "LAAAAAH," "MAAAAAA," or "SAAAAA." This could take only a minute or two or may extend up to 31 minutes. Working with mantra and sound begins to balance the manamaya kosha (the emotional or sensory mind) in the Panchamaya therapeutic model.

o **Relaxation and Meditation**

Up to this point of the session, the preparation is almost the same for a listener to now enter a state of yogic meditation or relaxation with the gong as in a regular yoga class environment. Indeed, this is often how Gong Yoga is practiced and we could simply begin to play the gong at this point as the listener meditated or relaxed and achieve good results.

In the Gong Yoga Therapy model, however, there is another phase that appears to be crucial in achieving a self-directed therapeutic change: the practice of Yoga Nidra, or yogic sleep.

o **Yoga Nidra**

Upon entering relaxation after a yoga practice, the participants are ready to experience the therapeutic state of Yoga Nidra, or "yogic sleep." In this state of directed awareness, healing and re-integration occurs on the subconscious level as well as the unconscious level.

The Yogis use the technique of Yoga Nidra to purify the deep impressions of the individual's "samskaras," the driving and usually hidden karmic forces behind many of our actions and conditions. Essentially, the state of Yoga Nidra gives access to the mind that is underneath our normal processing, fantasizing and imaging consciousness. It is an excellent tool for attenuating and eliminating habit patterns that are often the root causes of physical and psychological problems.

A Yoga Nidra session may last as little as 10 to 20 minutes or as long as an hour. Learning to practice and teach Yoga Nidra can be learned from several books on the subject but the methods essentially follow these guidelines:

- Setting an Intention–At the beginning of a Yoga Nidra practice, the participant should select a precise, clear and positive intention or resolve for the session. This positive resolve is known as a "sankalpa." The Sanskrit word means a resolution, free will or determination and is a basic tool in initiating a yogic healing process to awaken innate healing energies. A typical sankalpa might be, "I experience complete health," or "I am free of all pain."
- Awareness of Body–While in a state of relaxation after setting the intention, the participant's awareness is systematically directed to the different parts of the body. By rotating the awareness through all areas of the body in an automatic and spontaneous fashion, a body-mind state is created that begins the process of integration. Generally, a specific sequence is used to direct body awareness, beginning with the right hand, the right side, moving to the left side, to the back of the body, to the front of the body, the head, face, and back down to the legs. Books on Yoga Nidra have exact rotation of consciousness sequences to follow.
- Awareness of Breath–After the rotation of consciousness, an awareness of the breath is established, either through counting or breathing into different areas or points on the body. This awakens the flow of prana and energy to every cell in the body.
- Awareness of Feelings and Sensations–Now feelings and emotions are awakened, experienced, and removed through a directed focusing on pair of opposites, such as hot and cold, joy and sadness, love and fear, light and dark. This contrasting of opposites through words or imagery allows for emotional balancing and relaxation and integration of the brain hemispheres.
- Guided Visualization–The last stage of Yoga Nidra involves visualizations by the participant based upon suggestions from the instructor. These images usually have universal significance and are archetypal in nature (oceans, mountains, flowers, powerful symbols or iconic figures). These images or guided journey may have a definite relationship to the theme of the Gong Yoga Therapy session, such as healing the heart or experiencing forgiveness. This visualization develops concentration and dissolves the distinctions between the conscious and unconscious mind, allowing it to completely relax. In this deeply relaxed state, the next phase of Gong Therapy begins.

- **The Sound of the Gong**

   The gong is now introduced during the deep state of Yoga Nidra. Again depending upon the intent of the therapeutic session, the gong may be played in different ways and for various purposes. Several build and release cycles can release fears, for example, or a gentle pulsing around the heart area of the gong can release old emotions. This is where the intuitive ability of the Gong Yoga Therapist plays to the needs of the participant or group. Typically the gong would be played for a minimum of 10 to 15 minutes and as long as 30 minutes to an hour. Be aware that participants at this stage of the therapy session are in a vastly altered and receptive state of consciousness and no one should enter or leave the room at this time.

- **Closing the Session**

   With the last strike of the gong, silence ensues for one to several minutes. Very gently the participants are brought back into their breath and body and then reminded of their original intention, or sankalpa, for the session. They mentally repeat their resolve several times. The session is ended by having the participants gently move the hands and feet and stretch the bodies. Have them take their time coming slowly up to a seated posture. Close the session with a sound, a mantra, a prayer or a blessing. Have them open their eyes.

- **Re-Mapping and Integration**

   For most people, this will be a profound and deeply moving experience. Depending upon the group, they can share their experiences with a partner or each other or with the instructor. All who listen should just listen without judgment or comment. They may also write or draw about their experience to help process it. Before leaving, there should be time for normal human conversation and sharing in some light refreshments to help ground the participants. They should remain in the room in this awakened state for at least 15 minutes before leaving.

How to Play the Gong: Basic Playing Techniques

The gong is not a musical instrument.
The gong is God. So it is said; so it is.

Yogi Bhajan

Playing the gong in yoga is unlike playing most musical instruments. The purpose is not to entertain but to transport the listener into a non-ordinary realm of being where reintegration can occur. Consequently, the concepts of melodies, compositions, musical sequences, musical notes and pitch are not part of learning how to play the gong for yoga, meditation and healing. While the gong can be orchestrated for musical compositions, we are approaching how to play the gong as a yogic or therapeutic tool and not as a musical instrument. As a result, you do need any formal musical background or training to play the gong.

Playing the gong in yoga ultimately becomes a free-form expression of the intuitive state of the player that is completely unique and often irreproducible. When playing the gong for meditation, relaxation, healing and yogic transformation, the player does not read music, follow a score, or even work within a musical framework with other musicians. The gong is played alone, its voice so powerful only other gongs may join, as it follows a path more discovered than guided by its player.

Learning to play the gong is about learning to let the gong play you. While you need to understand the basic techniques, you also need to learn to listen to what the gong requires and drop the performer's ego. Rather than using the lower mind that seeks to please the performer and the audience, you will need to learn to listen to your discerning intelligence (what the yogis call the buddhi mind) so you can guide each stroke of the mallet in the perfect sequence of the moment.

Learning the techniques to play the gong is relatively simple compared to most other musical instruments. You can learn the basics in a matter of hours. Developing the intuitive state of mind to play it effectively, however, requires that the gong practitioner be in that state of yoga and integration that only comes from a dedicated personal practice of self-transformation.

Getting Started

There are three things needed to play the gong: the gong itself, a support or stand for the gong (although some small gongs can be held by hand), and a beater or mallet to strike the gong.

Assuming you have the gong supported with a proper stand and you have a mallet appropriate for the gong size and that the gong is positioned so it can move freely when played (see the section on Selection and Care of the Gong), you are ready to assume your playing position. You may wish to remove watches, rings and bracelets before playing the gong as sometimes these may brush against and scar the gong. Removing the shoes is also recommended and some players find that covering the head may help focus the energy that is released when playing a gong.

Approaching the Gong

The playing of the gong begins before the first strike. When used for yoga, meditation, and healing, the gong is a sacred instrument. All the master players throughout the ages respected the power of the sound of the gong. The attitude and the intention of the player were as important as any playing techniques or sequences. Consequently the gong was approached as an agent of divine transformation. It was considered a privilege to be able to play the gong and both give and receive its healing energy. The gong was played with respect for its power, not as a way to make a loud or impressive sound. While you may be playful with the gong, do not play around with the gong or allow it to be struck inappropriately.

To begin any gong playing session, center yourself with meditation, prayer, mantra or conscious intention. Take a moment to feel the presence of both yourself and the gong and the relationship between you and the instrument. Allow for the opportunity for the gong to guide you, to lead you, and to let you create the sounds that it wishes to express through you at this moment in time.

Playing Position

If the gong is on a floor stand, you will sit next to it. If it is suspended from a vertical stand, you will stand next to it. Sit or stand to the side so that your playing arm (depending if you are right or left-handed) can reach across the body to strike the front of the gong. In other words, you do not want the playing arm directly adjacent to the gong.

Come slightly forward from the gong so you can turn in toward it. You are partially facing into it but not blocking it. You should be close enough so that the playing arm can comfortably reach the farthest side of the gong with the elbow still slightly bent. You should not have to unduly stretch or change your position to reach any part of the gong. A common error for beginners is to sit or stand too far back. You need to be able to position yourself forward and angled enough from the side of the stand so you can see and reach all the playing areas.

Holding the Mallet

Gong mallets tend to feel heavy to the beginner and you will need to build strength in your arm and wrist to play for an extended length of time.

The mallet should be gripped so its weight can be manipulated with the wrist. Depending upon the size of the mallet, you may need to choke up on the handle as much as halfway to the head. As your strength develops, you can grip the mallet about two-thirds or more down from the head. You should hold the mallet so there is a floating sense of balance as you move the arm and ultimately the mallet will feel almost weightless.

Priming the Gong

Before you strike the gong with the mallet, the gong should be set into motion by tapping the gong inaudibly several times with the mallet or finger near its edge. It does not take much effort; some of the largest temple gongs in Japan are first "warmed," or set in vibration, merely by the moistened thumb of the priest.

This gentle tapping or priming is necessary, however, to set the gong into vibration. If the gong is struck without priming, the energy of the first stroke is expended into bringing the instrument into vibration. Consequently, the initial sound will not be warm and full-bodied.

Striking the Gong

The musical term for hitting a percussion instrument like the gong with a mallet is called the "attack." This word is best understood by looking at its origin that initially comes from the root word that means to "attach" or connect. Rather than thinking of the "attack" as being an aggressive action by one object on the other, it is really about attaching, or joining the mallet to the gong. How we attach or "yoke" (yoga) the mallet with the gong determines if we have a seamless merger into a union or an ungraceful marriage of sound maker (mallet) and sound producer (gong).

The important thing is that there is never a direct "attack" with the mallet to the gong. You never strike the gong dead-on or straight in with the mallet. A direct hit to the gong by the mallet produces a shattering and alarming sound. It destroys the overtones and deadens the movement.

Instead, the mallet is allowed to gently deflect off the gong surface at the moment of attack (or attachment) in order to produce a fuller sound. As the mallet head approaches the gong, it is turned slightly upward or downward by the wrist to produce a glancing blow, almost as if it were rebounding off the gong surface. This creates a freedom of movement since the mallet head is not holding tightly to the surface and the proper overtones can develop.

Similarly, the gong is never struck in the exact center with the mallet as this also deadens the movement and destroys the overtones. When striking toward the center, the mallet moves off-center at the time of impact and again with a glancing blow.

The movement of the mallet generally comes from the shoulder and the wrist. The elbow may be bent or peripherally involved but the movement never comes directly from the elbow as this creates a pounding sound that is difficult to control. The mallet moves in a gentle arc from the shoulder that terminates in a smaller arc by the wrist right before impact.

While the shoulder movement can control the loudness of the sound, the arc in the wrist is the most important part of the movement as this controls the quality sound that is produced. The angle of the wrist arc is the fundamental way the gong is controlled and played.

The angle of the mallet head may move upward in the glancing blow or downward as it strikes the gong. This upward and downward stroking is significant as you learn to make the different sounds. For now, just be aware that the mallet may move in either direction as it encounters the gong.

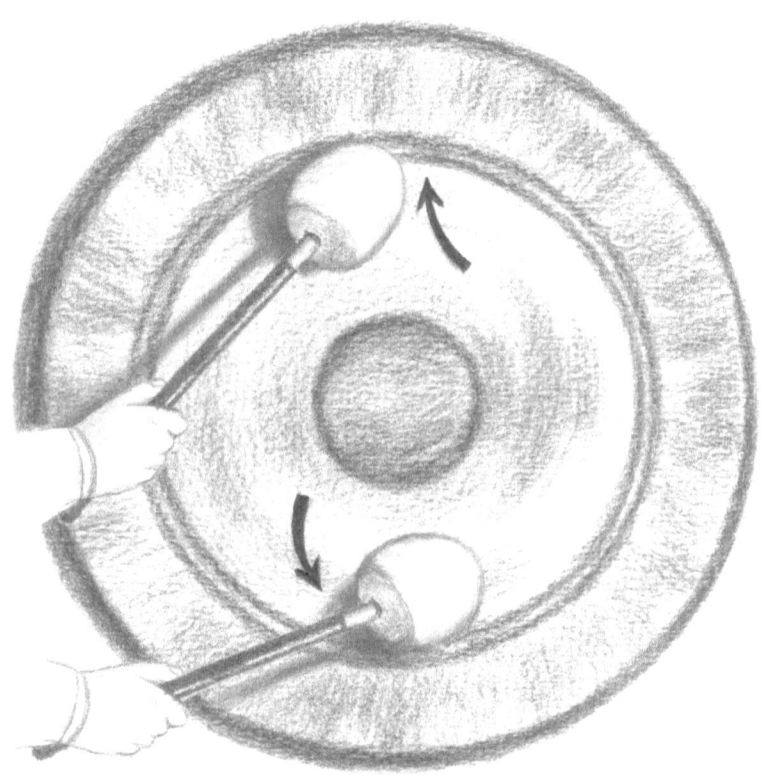

HOW TO STRIKE THE GONG

The mallet strikes with an upward angle on an up stroke by slightly turning the wrist up before the moment of impact. The mallet strikes with a downward angle on a down stroke by slightly turning the wrist down before the moment of impact.

PRACTICE SESSION #1:
The Mallet Stroke

In this session you will practice the basic mallet stroke. Position and hold the mallet so it can be easily turned by the wrist.

Practice: The Up Stroke
Begin by playing on the upper half of the gong that is farthest from you. As you swing the mallet toward the gong, move it in a small upward arc with the wrist as it strikes the surface. The wrist turns upward and the closed hand faces the sky. Do this several times, so the blow feels almost like a light glancing rebound. It is not necessary to strike hard or maintain contact with the surface. As you practice this upward stroke, begin to vary how much you turn or move the wrist. Feel free to move and reposition the body so you can turn easily into the gong.

Practice: The Down Stroke
Begin by playing on the lower half of the gong that is farthest from you. As you swing the mallet toward the gong, move it in a small downward arc with the wrist as it strikes the surface. The wrist turns downward and the closed hand faces the ground. Do this several times, so the blow feels almost like a light glancing rebound. Notice how the shoulder and arm movement differ slightly from an upward stroke. Remember it is not necessary to strike hard nor maintain contact with the surface. As you practice this downward stroke, begin to vary how much you turn or move the wrist. Feel free to move and reposition the body so you can turn easily into the gong.

Practice: Alternating Strokes
Now begin to alternate between an upward stroke on the top half of the gong with a downward stroke on the bottom half of the gong. Play a few inches above and below the midline. Adjust the body so that both strokes can be delivered comfortably. Begin to notice the different sounds produced by an up stroke and by a down stroke.

Practice: Stilling the Gong
To still the sound and movement of the gong, hold the mallet head snugly against the surface so the gong cannot move and the vibration is halted. This is called muffling the gong and is used to silence the sound. Practice muffling the gong at the end of your practice sessions.

Practice: Striking on approach
As your play the gong, you will notice a natural swing develops as it moves back and forth under the impact of the strokes. Begin to play the different areas of

the gong (center, mid-area and rim) until the gong enters into a natural swing. Now practice striking the gong as it moves toward you. Notice the sound this produces. Observe what happens to the intensity of the swing. Is the sound louder? Does the swing increase or decrease?

Practice: Striking on departure
Now begin to strike the gong on the swing as it moves away from you. Notice the sound this produces. Observe what happens to the intensity of the swing. Is the sound louder or less? Does the swing increase or decrease?

Practice: Stabilizing the gong
You may have noticed how the gong may sway too much side to side, wobble off center, or swing too much back and forth. When the gong begins to move erratically or extremely, you will not be able to control the quality of the sound and you will need to stabilize the movement and slow the swing. To stabilize the gong, strike the gong as it moves toward you with a slight contact of the mallet head against the surface. Strike the area that is moving the most (sides or top or bottom) and toward the rim to maximize the corrective torque.

The Playing Areas of the Gong

The surface of the gong is divided into three striking areas: center area, mid-area, and rim area. On some gongs, you can see these areas clearly delimited by the finish on the surface. The center area appears to be like a small sun with a diameter about one-quarter the size of the entire gong. The rim area is slightly rough and extends in just a few inches from the edge. The mid-area between the rim and the center is the largest playing area, sometimes colored between the darker rim and the brighter center. Each playing area produces a different quality of sound when struck.

While all these areas may be freely played, the gong should never be struck on the exact outer edge of the rim or directly dead center. Remember the center area is always struck slightly off true center (the only exception to this is a tuned gong that is "bossed" with an elevated center).

Striking the gong near the center area gives a rich, enduring and carrying sound–almost like a strong fundamental note. Striking in the mid-area between the center and rim produces a deep, complete and swelling sound–rich and complex in tone coloring. Striking in the rim area gives an airy, sparkling and roaring sound–partial tones that transcend any specific pitch.

While gongs are generally struck over all three areas to produce a wide variety of sound, each gong has one or more ideal striking spots that produce its most characteristic and optimal sound quality. This striking spots are sometimes referred to as the "sweet spots" where a strike by the mallet produces a most pleasing sound. The position of this "sweet spot" varies from gong to gong and may be dependent on the size and tuning of the gong as well as its individual manufacture. Typically, however, the sweet spot is generally found in the lower triangle of the mid-area of the gong.

As the gong is played, it will begin to naturally move back and forth (and sometimes side to side) in a rhythmical dance. Should the swing or movement become exaggerated or difficult to control, the movement can be slowed by striking the area of the gong as it moves toward you on its approach. Again, the strike should be a deflecting blow, not straight on.

If you want to increase the loudness of the sound, strike the gong as it comes toward you. To lessen the loudness, time the stroke to hit the gong as it moves away from you.

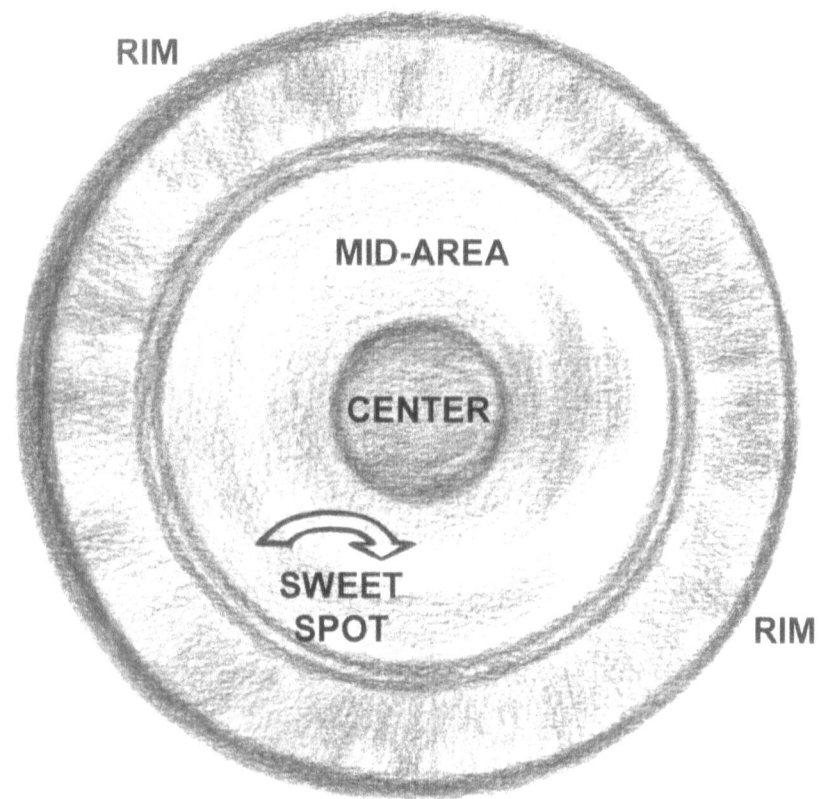

THE PLAYING AREAS OF THE GONG

The three standard playing areas of the gong and a designated "sweet spot" area that often varies from gong to gong.

Practice Session #2: Exploring the Areas of the Gong

In this session you learn about striking different areas of the gong and the resulting sounds.

Practice: Exploring the Center, Mid-Area and Rim

Assume your position by the gong and touch the center, mid-area, and rim with the mallet head. Begin by striking at the top of the center area (right before it becomes the mid-area) with an upward mallet stroke. Alternate with a downward mallet stroke at the bottom edge of the center area. Move the mallet back and forth, from top center to bottom center, with an up stroke at top center and a bottom stroke at the bottom center. Listen to the sound produced at the center of the gong and how the top center sound differs from the bottom center sound. Remember to never strike the gong dead center. Now muffle the gong by holding the head at the center.

Explore the mid-area by striking the mallet between the center and the rim. Use an upward mallet stroke in the top mid-area and a bottom stroke in the bottom half of the mid-area. Move all around the mid area, in and out from the circle and rim, and listen to the quality of sound that is produced. After awhile muffle the gong by holding the head at the center.

Now move to the rim of the gong. While some advanced players can strike the edge of the rim for a specific effect, beginners should play the inside edge of the rim. Begin playing the inside rim area farthest from you, again using an upward mallet stroke on the top half of the gong and a bottom stroke on the bottom half of the gong. Move completely around the rim several times and then alternate clockwise and counterclockwise. When you are finished muffle the gong by holding the head at the center.

Practice: Finding the Sweet Spot

Assume your position by the gong and locate the lower third mid-area region of the gong. Explore this region by striking the gong with a single stroke at a time and fully listen to the sound it produces. Then move a few inches from the last stroke and strike again. Continue to play around the lower mid-area on both sides of the gong until you discover which place produces the fullest, richest and most resonant sound when struck. This is the "sweet spot." Muffle the gong and now begin to practice striking the sweet spot with varying strengths and rhythms and listen to the sound as it swells. You may be able to locate a second "sweet spot" on your gong in other areas. Generally, the sweet spot of a gong is generally around two-thirds out from the center and toward the bottom.

Percussion Points

Now that you have experienced the three major areas of the gong, you can explore specific playing spots on the gong known as percussion points. A percussion point produces a distinctive sound when struck. These percussion points are the same on all gongs and serve as a reference point to indicate where a mallet should strike.

Think of the gong as a clock face divided into 12 areas, one for each hour. The 12 o'clock position is at the top of the gong (or more precisely in the top of the mid-area of the gong below the rim). The 6 o'clock position is at the bottom, again above the rim area. The other clock positions go around the outer mid-area of gong so there are 12 points or localized areas that can be struck. In the middle of the gong, there is a zero position so that the upper center area (before the mid-area begins) is known as "Up 0" and the lower center area is known as "Down 0." So we now have 14 total percussion points on the gong (including the two center "0" points) where the vast majority of the mallet strikes will occur.

As you play these points, you will discover that each produces a different sound quality and when sequenced appropriately will create a complementary wall of sound.

GONG PERCUSSION POINTS

The specific playing points on a gong (percussion points) are designated as a clock face with two center points, Up 0 and Down 0.

For the beginning player, it is useful to think of the percussion points of the gong as being divided by a horizontal axis, across the face of the "clock" from point 3 to 9. The points above the horizontal center (1, 2, 10, 11, 12) are generally played with an up stroke of the mallet. The points below the horizontal center (4, 5, 6, 7, 8) are generally played with a down stroke of the mallet. The two mid-horizontal points (3 and 9) are played up or down depending upon the gong player's left-hand or right-hand orientation. If right-handed, the point 9 is played with a down stroke and point 3 is played with an up stroke. You may reverse the up and down stroke if you are a left-handed player. The Down 0 point, just below center, is played with a down stroke and the Up 0 point, just above the center, is played with an up stroke.

These "up" and "down" strokes based on percussion points are very helpful as you learn to play the gong. As you understand how to work with the sound of the gong, you may reverse the up and down strokes to achieve a particular effect at a percussion point. For example, when you play a traditionally "down" stroke percussion point with an "up" stoke instead, you change the quality of its energy by raising its frequency. Similarly a "down" stroke played on a normally "up" stroke percussion point will lower its frequency when that such an effect is needed.

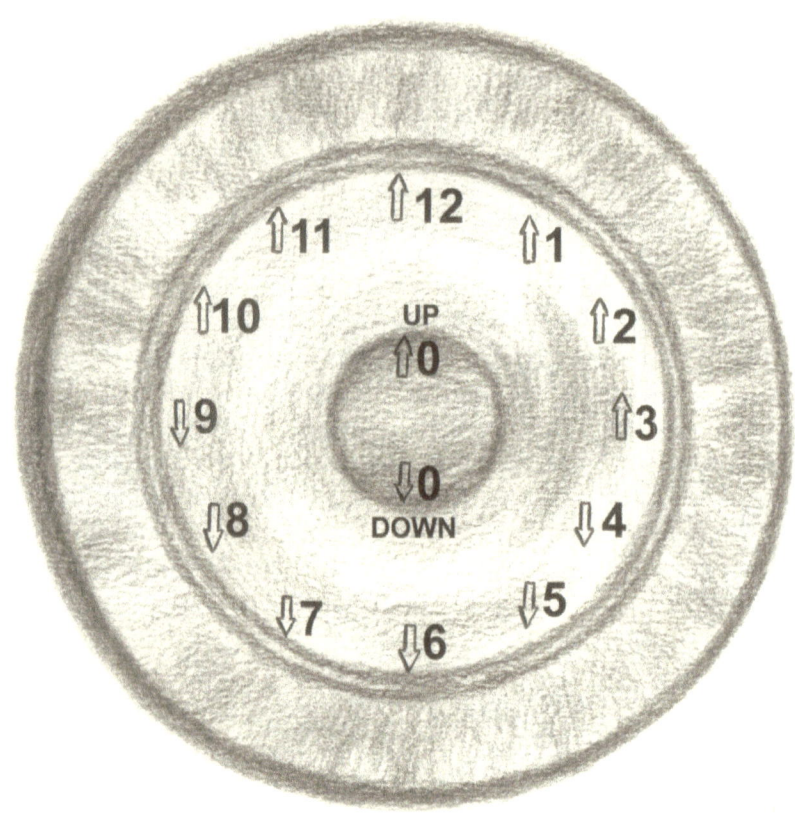

PERCUSSION POINTS AND MALLET STRIKE DIRECTION

Each percussion point is associated with an upward mallet strike, indicated by an up arrow next to the number, or a downward strike, indicated by a downward arrow next to the number. Note that there is both an upward strike and downwawrd strike associated with the two central "0" points.

Practice Session #3:
Playing the Percussion Points

In this practice session you will become familiar with the mallet strokes for the different percussion points.

Practice: Up Stroke Points
Assume your position and locate the "up" stroke points on the gong: points 1, 2, 3, 10, 11, 12. Now strike each of these percussion points with an up stroke as you move around the gong in no particular order. Listen to the sound each percussion point produces and become comfortable using an up stroke on these areas.

Practice: Down Stroke Points
Muffle the gong and now locate the "down" stroke points on the gong: points 4, 5, 6, 7, 8, 9. Now strike each of these percussion points with a down stroke as you move around the gong in no particular order. Listen to the sound that each percussion point produces and become comfortable using a down stroke on these areas.

Practice: Center Points
Muffle the gong and locate the 0 percussion points on the gong–points 0 Top (at the top of the center area) and point 0 Bottom (at the bottom of the center area). Now strike the 0 Top point with an up stroke and then play the 0 Bottom point with a down stroke. Listen to the subtle difference in sound each 0 point produces and begin to alternate playing the 0 Top and the 0 Bottom points with up strokes and down strokes.

Designating a Sequence of Strokes
The percussion points give us the beginning of a musical language to describe how to play the gong. For example, if we wish to play percussion point 3 and then strike percussion point 6, we can denote that with the sequence "3–6." In this way the percussion points are used to indicate mallet placement and take the place of standard musical notation.

Another example, if we wanted to first strike the gong at the 2 percussion point position, then at the 8 position, then strike 2 again and then 8 again, and finally end with a strike at the 6 position, you would denote this playing sequence as 2-8-2-8-6.

The two 0 center percussion points are distinguished as 0-Up and 0-Down so an alternation between playing these two points would be specified as "0-Up-0-Down-0-Up-0-Down." Remember that all the other percussion points have an associated default up or down stroke that need not be explicitly specified. Point

12 with a normal up stroke is simply specified as "12." If we wanted to reverse the normal up stroke on point 12 and strike this point instead with a down stroke then we would explicitly specify that as "12-Down."

We will use the percussion point notation throughout this and the next chapter to indicate where to strike the gong as you practice.

Creating a Sound Sequence

When playing the gong, there is always a formal or intuitive sequencing of strokes at all times. There are no "random" strokes as each successive stroke must enhance, complement, contrast, or support the previous stroke. Without an applied or native sequence, you are just banging the gong.

In general, most gong playing consists of multiple short sequences woven together throughout the session. While you could compose a 30-minute playing session meticulously arranged as a complex sequence of hundreds of percussion point strikes, in reality this does not reflect the real-time composition and intuitive playing of most gong players. Most playing is built around sequences of 1 to 8 percussion points that are repeated throughout the session.

As you learn to play more from your intuitive state, you will "discover" new sequences that you will automatically employ in your state of spontaneous playing. Think of these sequences as phrases or mantras of individual sounds that work together to create an effect that come into the player's consciousness as needed.

Practice Session #4: Playing Sequences

To develop an intuitive sequencing ability that comes from experience, let's look at some standard sequences you can practice to gain dexterity and understanding.

Practice: Playing Around the Face

A simple way to build a sequence is to play around the face of the gong on the four major percussion points 3, 6, 9 and 12. This is a balancing sequence that calls into play the four major sounding areas. Playing around the face of the gong with this sequence has the effect of building and gathering energy. The playing sequence is denoted as "9-6-3-12." In other words, you strike the 9 percussion point first, then 6, then 3, and finally 12. Use the appropriate upward or downward strokes (9 down, 6 down, 3 up, 12 up) and begin to play around the face of the gong with this four percussion point sequence.

GONG PLAYING SEQUENCE

The arrows next to the percussion points illustrate how each point is struck with a downward or upward mallet stroke. This simple four percussion point sequence of 9-6-3-12 illustrates how to play around the face of the gong.

Practice: Playing the Diagonal Points

Now play the diagonal points on the gong. The primary diagonal point sequences are 2 and 8 ("2–8") and 10 and 4 ("10–4") with the 1–7 and 11–5 point pairs the secondary diagonal sequences. Playing diagonal point sequences can have the effect of releasing and moving blocked energy. First strike 2 (upward) and then 8 (downward). After a few repetitions, play 10 (upward) and then 4 (downward) for a few cycles. Sometimes playing diagonal points strongly can cause the gong to wobble and produce a "wha-wha" feedback sound that can be effective to create the experience of expansion and contraction. Alternatively, it can also create an out of balance movement that may be difficult to control so proceed cautiously with enthusiastic diagonal point playing. Finally, alternate playing the "2–8" sequence and the "10–4" sequence for a few cycles. These are typical 2 percussion point sequences, one of the most common building blocks in creating sequences.

Practice: Multiple Strikes on Single Points

Quite commonly the same percussion point may form a sequence by itself with multiple strikes. This is an effective way to lock the mind and direct energy. The longer this sequence is held, the more powerful it can become or, when overextended, ultimately draining. Generally a multiple strike on a single percussion point lasts for 2 to 8 strikes. For maximum contrast in sound, play points 6 and 12 in this way: "6-6-6-6" and then "12-12-12-12." Try each sequence individually and then alternate the two sequences. Now use a 2 strike sequence on points 3 and 9 in this way: "9–9" and then "3–3." Play them individually for a few cycles and then alternate these two stroke sequences.

Practice: Putting Sequences Together

Now let's take several sequences and link them together. Play these percussion point sequences in this order:

9-6-3-12
0-Up-0-Down
9-6-3-12
12-12-12-12
0-Up-0-Down
6-6-6-6-6-6-6-6

If you want to extend this practice, repeat each sequence 2 to 4 times before playing the next sequence. Vary the number of repetitions for different sequences and experience the sound it creates.

Loudness and Volume

The sound of the gong depends primarily on where it is struck (percussion points and playing areas) and how it is struck (loudness and rhythm).

Loudness is generally an effect of the strength of the attack and (as we mentioned earlier) if the gong is moving toward or away from the mallet. The mallet head itself can also affect loudness. A harder head produces a sharper (and louder) sound than a padded head. Some players have both types of mallets to regulate the loudness.

A common mistake made by beginners is to play too loudly as they misjudge the effect of the impact and how it can build quickly with the movement of the gong. In general, it is better to underplay than overplay the gong while in the learning stage. On the other hand, a suitably strong played gong can have deep therapeutic effects so knowing how and when to increase the loudness is essential.

The most effective way to build loudness is through repeated strokes on the same point and allowing the natural wave of sound to increase on its own. This repeated stroking builds a constant level of loudness that becomes self-sustaining. On other hand, a well-directed and powerfully placed single stroke can create a punctuation point of loudness that takes the listener to a completely new realm of sound and being. This "thunderbolt" approach to playing can be extremely effective when done correctly. It can also be extremely shattering and detrimental when done inappropriately. Remember that for most people, the gong already sounds loud simply because of its strong presence so proceed judiciously with your volume.

Practice Session #5: Controlling Volume

Let's experiment with creating different sound experiences by learning to control the volume of the sound of the gong through several techniques.

Practice: Controlling Volume through the Strike
Locate the sweet spot on your gong and strike softly. Let the sound die away naturally. Wait until there is almost silence. Now strike the same spot again with a slightly stronger stroke (remember that the mallet always strikes at an angle to the gong face and never dead on). Let the sound swell and decay naturally. Notice how the sound waves last a little longer. Now strike the same spot forcefully. Again experience the swelling and decaying of the sound.

Move the mallet to another percussion point of your choice and repeat the sequence: soft strike, firm strike, and hard strike.

Now go around the face of the gong and strike the 3-6-9-12 percussion points softly in sequence. Repeat several times around the 3-6-9-12 points with a light strike.

Continue this sequence with a firm strike now on these points. Try to keep the rhythm or speed the same.

Now muffle the gong and begin the 3-6-9-12 playing sequence with a somewhat forceful strike. Notice how the loudness can easily get away from you as the sound builds on its on. Muffle the gong when you need to do so.

Over time, you will discover the proper force of a strike to produce the loudness you intend.

Practice: Controlling Volume through Repetition
Select a single percussion point to play over and over again with a soft strike, almost like you are feathering the gong. Keep a steady rate without varying the speed or rhythm. Notice how the repeated strikes will build loudness over time. Increase the strength of the stroke and continue to repeatedly strike the same spot. Muffle the gong and then move to other percussion points and repeat the strokes at a steady rate to increase the loudness. Notice how you can quickly build loudness through repetition without increasing the strength of the stroke.

Now let's practice increasing and decreasing the strength of the stroke as you strike the same spot over and over. Play one spot with a firm rhythm until it reaches a state of moderate loudness. Now begin to softly strike the same spot over and over. After awhile you will begin to diminish the loudness by repeated soft strikes. A softer strike on a spot can actually diminish the sound created by a firmer strike. Try this over several areas of the gong.

It is important to experience how a properly placed strike or repeated strikes can be used to still the gong from a louder vibration. This is an important technique to practice because it allows you to move loudness up and down in a dynamic way without having to muffle a gong. This ability to both increase and decrease loudness through repeated strikes is a valuable tool to have as we move into the advanced playing techniques.

Practice: The Thunderbolt Strike
A powerful sound can be created by a single strong strike to the gong, much like a lightning strike that releases the sound of thunder. Like lightning, the thunderbolt strike is most effective when it is done with a sharp decisive quick hit. It should be delivered when the gong is in motion and moving toward

you. A thunderbolt strike on a still gong can shatter and scatter the energy and sound and should be avoided. As this is the "loudest" volume obtainable with the gong, it must be used wisely and in contrast to other sound levels.

Begin with a soft to firm strike on the percussion points around the face of the gong, 3-6-9-12. After several repetitions of this playing sequence, deliver a strong single strike above the center of the gong (the 0-Up percussion point). Immediately move back into the 3-6-9-12 playing sequence for three more repetitions and then a thunderbolt strike to below the center area of the gong (the 0-Down percussion point).

Practice in this manner by playing the 3-6-9-12 sequence for several repetitions and alternating a thunderbolt strike between the 0-Up and the 0-Down positions. Remember that the mallet head always strikes at a slight angle or arc and never directly dead-on. This is especially important with the thunderbolt strike.

Another way to practice is to play the 2–8 diagonal points over and over with a light to firm stroke and then hitting both points with a thunderbolt strike in rapid succession. As a general rule, the thunderbolt strike is rarely delivered to the same spot in rapid succession because it primarily works through contrast in either loudness or position and its impact is diminished when it is sustained.

It will take practice and experience to deliver the thunderbolt stroke effectively and should only be gradually introduced into a public playing session as you become proficient and confident.

Rhythm Rates

Along with loudness, the rhythm or speed of the strokes determine the quality and effect of the sound of the gong. In general, a rapid rhythm raises energy and intensifies the experience of the listener. A slower rhythm releases tension and relaxes the mind. Usually the gong player varies the rhythm as the playing sequences change. In general, a gong playing session begins with a slow rhythm to allow the listener to easily enter the sound. Over time, the rhythm may increase as energy is moved and shifted and then slowed down to ground the listener as the session ends.

It is the rhythm of the strokes that is the key to creating the complex combination tones that is unique to the gong. An overly ambitious rhythm can step on the sound and not allow the tones to work together. An inappropriately played slow rhythm can drain away the overtones and inhibit developing a rich complexity that profoundly affects the consciousness. This proper rhythm cannot be taught but only experienced through repeated practice as it varies according to each sequence. In general, most players use a range of rhythms throughout a gong playing session.

Perhaps some of the most advanced gong players in the world are those who play in the Gamelan orchestras of the Far East, a collection of gong-related percussion instruments. The entire structure of their music is marked by the rhythm maintained by the largest gong in the orchestra and the space between its two gong strokes is the fundamental music unit known as a "gongan."

Remember that the gong is a percussion instrument and the rhythm at which it is played (or its "gongan") is one of the most crucial factors in creating an appropriate sound experience. Just as we arbitrarily describe a mallet strike as soft, firm and hard, let's practice a relational range of slow, moderate, and fast rhythms on the gong.

Practice Session #6: Working with Rhythms

In this session we will explore how to change rhythm rates, work with rhythms in sequences, and the relationship of rhythm to sound and effect.

Practice: Establishing Rhythm Rate

Play percussion point 3 on the gong face with a slow steady rhythm with a light to firm strike. Now increase the tempo of the strokes by about 25% and hold to this rhythm. As you increase the tempo of the strokes, keep the striking pressure the same (light to firm). After awhile, increase the rate another 25%. Again increase the rhythm another 25% and continue building the tempo until you feel you are at your highest sustained rate. Then begin to reduce the tempo 25% at a step until you move back to your initial slow rhythm.

What happened to the volume of the gong? How did the gong move? What difficulties did you experience with increasing the tempo? Could you find a rhythm rate that allowed the sound of the gong to be expressed most fully? What internal changes did you experience with an increased rhythm rate?

Now move back to the face of the gong with the 9-6-3-12 percussion point sequence. Begin again with a slow rhythm as you play these points and gradually increase the tempo until you discover a rate that allows the sound to express itself fully. Too slow and the tones drag, too fast and the tones crash on top of each other.

Use both rhythm and repeated striking points to create a pleasant swell of volume. Work with the up stroke on percussion point 12 at the top of the gong face. As you continue to strike this point, gradually increase only the rhythm rate until it is a moderately fast tempo. The volume should increase accordingly. Muffle the gong and begin again, repeating the strikes at point 12 and then increasing the striking force while also accelerating the rhythm. Build to a rapid tempo with firm strokes and note the intensity of the sound.

Now muffle the gong and move down to point 6 at the bottom of the gong face and begin a repeated down strike with a moderate rhythm and firm strike. Slow only the rhythm but keep the stroke firm. Now soften the strike and keep the slow rhythm at point 6. Notice the quality and volume of the sound. Contrast the experience of playing the two percussion points with an increasing or decreasing rhythm. Note how a fast rhythm at point 12 seems to almost lift the energy out of the body while a slow rhythm at point 6 creates a deep grounding sound.

Practice: Rhythm Rate Variations with Sequences
Let's vary the rhythm now according to sequences. This is often how you will experience playing the gong in an extended session.

Begin with a slow rhythm playing the standard sequence of percussion points 9-6-3-12. Unless otherwise noted, use a moderate light to firm strike throughout this practice. Play this sequence for about 1 minute.

Now move immediately into a 9–3 sequence with a slightly faster rhythm. Play this sequence for 30 seconds.

Return to the slower rhythm around the 9-6-3-12 points again for 30 seconds. Continue this slow rhythm and move to 0-Up-0-Down sequence for 1 minute.

Now move play points 2–8 beginning with the same slow rhythm and gradually picking up the tempo over 1 to 2 minutes until you are playing at your most proficient fast rhythm.

Give a single thunderbolt strike at 0-Up and then 0-Down.

Return to the fast rhythm of 2–8 for 30 seconds.

Another thunderbolt strike to 0-Up and then 0-Down.

Slow the rhythm down as you return to 9-6-3-12 for 1 minute.

Stay at percussion point 6, slowing the tempo and lighting the stroke, for 2 minutes.

Finish with a slightly firmer strike to 0-Up-0-Down-0-Up-0-Down and again to 0-Down.

This whole practice will take about 10 minutes. You may feel the strain of the extended playing until your arm gets used to the weight of the mallet. When beginning, limit your practice sessions to 10 minutes with breaks in between. Be aware that the sound of the gong produces an altered state of consciousness on the player as well.

Continuing Your Practice

You now have the basic techniques to practice with the gong. Practicing on the gong is unlike practicing with another musical instrument. While you can certainly work on the basics of percussion points, rhythm rates and sequencing, you also need to work on your own consciousness.

Playing the gong itself is a conscious-changing act. It requires a subtlety and understanding that only comes when the player is in that state of higher consciousness. You will not be able to play any higher than your own state of being. To be a better gong player, you must also be a better yogi.

Practice will often be most productive after you have practiced your own yoga and meditation. It is essential so that you can enter that intuitive state where true playing comes from. If you do not have time for a lengthy practice, at least take the time to control your own prana, your own breath and energy, with a simple breathing exercise like alternate nostril breathing before your begin your practice.

You will discover the gong actually plays you more than you play the gong. Make yourself that pure instrument, that pure channel, so the sacred sound of the gong can manifest through you.

How to Play the Gong: Advanced Playing Techniques

As you continue to develop your playing skills, you may wish to experiment with more advanced techniques. Many of these techniques come naturally over time. Some may take several years to feel effective. Be aware that technique is always secondary to intention and when the gong is played for healing and transformation, the ego should not be involved in pleasing the player or the listener by its real or imagined virtuosity as you master these advanced techniques.

Combination Strokes: Ties and Slurs

The gong player creates unique sound patterns by combining two or more strikes that may vary in duration and pitch to create a single blended unit of sound. For those who know music theory and notation, this is equivalent to "ties" (two notes of the same pitch connected) and "slurs" (two notes of different pitch) that are played together as one longer musical unit.

With the gong this is accomplished by a strike being followed immediately with a follow-up stroke to create the sound of a multiple beat. When struck on the same point this is a "tie." This multiple beat or "tie" is different from simply repeatedly striking the same point as we did in the basic playing technique section. The multiple strikes make one note, one playing sound, that is integrated into the overall rhythm.

A simple way to think of this "tie" technique is to make the combined strikes so close together they sound like almost one beat. A "tie" is typically two strikes but could also be three or four tied strikes.

The "slur" technique involves hitting different percussion points quickly in succession so that it becomes a singular rhythmical beat in the overall rhythm.

This is accomplished by skipping the mallet over the surface as it connects the two points together.

A simple way to think of the "slur" technique is to make the combined strikes in a gliding movement so that mallet head stays close to the playing surface as it moves to the next point. The need to keep the points close together to "slur" them limits how far apart on the surface each successive strike can be. However, many strikes could be slurred together in an almost "washboard" effects as you skip quickly around the surface to create a unique and powerful rhythm.

More complex combination stroke sequences can be built by first tying two stokes together and then slurring them. Or slurring two strokes which are followed with a tied strike at the end of the slur. You can even tie slurs together, or create a continuous slur around the gong where all the sounds are then tied together.

Practice Session #7: Combination Stokes

Practice a tie by first striking the 6 percussion point with two regular downward strikes and then striking the 4 percussion point. Now tie the two 6 strikes together with a rapid one-two strike and then strike the 4 point. The time you spend on the two 6 strikes should be equal to the time on the one 4 strike. It is as if the two 6 strikes are counted as one beat equal to the single beat 4 strike.

COMBINATION STROKE: THE TIE

In this example of a "tie" stroke, the player strikes percussion point 6 with two quick beats to tie them together as one beat and then strikes percussion point 4 as a single regular beat. Note the "tie" stroke occurs between the two beats on point 6.

Now play the around the face sequence of 9-6-3-12 again. Practice tying different points together. Strike the 9 percussion point with a double strike as one beat and then strike 6-3-12 with one strike and one beat. Tie the 6, 3, and 12 points with a double beat at each point. Now tie the 9 and 3 points with two quick strikes and strike the 6 and 12 points with a single strike.

Practice a tie of three strikes at the 6 point and single strikes at points 3-12-9. Go back and play some of the earlier sequences and experiment with tying strikes in the sequence and see how you change the sound.

Try a simple slur by striking the 7 percussion point and then the 6 percussion point. Move the mallet quickly so that the strike on the 7–6 points sound likes one beat, one sound. Now slur the 3 and 2 percussion points. Move the slur so you now strike percussion points 3 and 1 as a slur and then slur the 8 and 6 percussion points.

COMBINATION STROKE: THE SLUR

In this example of a "slur" stroke, the player strikes percussion point 6 and 7 with a quick sliding strike to meld them together as one beat.

For fun, try a slur and a tie. Slur percussion points 8 and 7 and then tie them to the 6 percussion point. Remember that the slurred points will have the same number of beats as the tied beat. You can even slur the 8 and 7 points to a doubled tied 6 percussion point!

Experiment with the combination tones, varying rhythm, repetition, and strength of the strike. Discovering how to create effective combination tones is one of the most important stages of a gong player's development.

Pulsing The Gong and Returning the Sound

The gong responds well to pulsing or building a rhythmical swelling of sound. This pulsing entrances the mind and creates an underlying focus for listening. It is an excellent technique to use to intrigue the listener and to lead them in and out of complex sound sequences.

The gong player creates pulsing by first establishing a steady rhythm with light to firm baseline strokes typically at one point. After several baseline strikes, a stronger dominant stroke is made at regular intervals. The "pulse" of the dominant stoke determines the tempo. Pulsing can be increased with a firmer strike of the dominant stroke or shortening the duration or number of lighter strikes between the dominant strokes. While all strikes in a pulsing sequence may be made on a single percussion point and thereby enhance its hypnologic effect, the dominant stroke may also be made in another area from the baseline strokes to create an accentuated sound.

Returning the Sound

When the gong is struck, up to 12 or 13 waves of sound may be produced. These waves build and return to create a rich and complex sound of overtones and combination tones.

A common mistake by beginning players is to "step on" or scatter the natural returning sound of the gong by playing too quickly or out of rhythm. Knowing how to produce and work with the returning sound is an important playing technique. Ideally, you will learn how to play in a rhythm that enhances and spotlights the returning sound. When done skillfully, the gong player can create a "humming" or "swishing" sound by building on these returning waves.

Practice Session #8: Creating Pulsing and Returning Sounds

Play the bottom of the gong at the 6 percussion point with a light steady rhythm. Vary the rhythm until you sense a building pulse of sound. Now begin to emphasize every fourth strike so there is a tempo in the pulsing sound, such as 6 (light)–6 (light)–6 (light)–6 (strong), 6 (light)–6 (light)–6 (light)–6 (strong), and so on.

Explore other areas of the gongs with different rhythm (faster, slower) and tempo rates (every third strike, sixth strike, etc.).

To experience the returning sound, play the 2 percussion point area with soft upstrokes. Experiment with the rhythm until you hear a "humming," "singing," or returning sound. Alternate between the 2 percussion point and 4 percussion point and see if you can create that returning swishing sound, then move to 9 and 3, and finally 2 and 8. Occasionally allow the sound to exist in space and hold off on the next strike. The pause between strikes becomes a powerful technique we will discuss later. For example, rather than a four-four rhythm like one, two, three, four, allow the fourth strike to be unstruck, so you play one, two, three, pause; one, two, three, pause.

Gong Songs: Building Sequences into Sessions

As you become familiar with how to build combination strokes over various percussion points, the next step is to learn to build the sequences that compose a gong playing session, or a gong song!

A sequence is simply one or more percussion points repeatedly played, either singularly or as combination strokes. Remember that a sequence generally consists of playing two to six percussion points and rarely exceeds twelve percussion points.

Beginning a Session

A gong session usually begins with a baseline of sound that builds a background for the combination tones to unfold. Generally, this may be something as simple as repeatedly playing a single percussion point until the sound begins to swell. A more complex baseline could be built by "tieing" a single point or slurring two points together to create a combination stroke for your baseline.

The purpose at the beginning of the session is to introduce the listener to the gong, create a sense of trust and involvement, and then establish a tone of expectancy, a setting of energy for the session to come. For example, a slow rhythm over a single percussion point creates a different expectation in the listener than a rapid slur between two points. Regardless, the opening baseline should be a launching point for the first sequence.

Typically the first sequence of a session is simple, perhaps 2 to 4 points played in a simple and predictable rhythm. The purpose of the first sequence is to educate the listener in how to listen to and follow the sound of the gong. Complexities and intricacies can come later.

Creating and Building Sequences

A session may consist of only one sequence or a multitude of non-repeating sequences. Typically, one or more sequences are often repeated in a session, much like a chorus or melody that revisits and reinforces the theme of the session.

Depending upon the length of the session, you may use several sequences individually or repeated together over and over. You could, for example, play a very simple sequence with variation in loudness over and over again for an entire session. In general, a session usually consists of several playing sequences that have a complementary and synergistic relationship with each other so that each leads naturally into the next to create a cumulative effect.

Playing sequences are often discovered rather than invented. As you experiment and play with the gong, you will discover sequences of playing points that work well together and they will become part of your gong playing background.

Do not be intimidated by the sequencing. As you learn to play from your intuitive center, you will play sequences by ear, automatically moving effortlessly from point to point, sequence to sequence. Just as the individual percussion points become second nature to you, so will standard sequences that you will return to seamlessly again and again.

Ending a Session

The last sequence of the session leads to the most important strokes in a gong playing session: the last stroke (ultimate) and the next-to-last stroke (penultimate).

The ultimate stroke should be integrating, sealing and grounding. It should signal to the listener that the session has ended, the sacred space is closed, and a transition is coming. The ultimate stroke should be definite and not tentative (although not necessarily loud). There should not be a sense of a stroke still waiting to be delivered after the last strike. There must be an expression of finality. Otherwise the listener may be disoriented. Depending on how you wish to leave the energy, the ultimate stroke can be made upwards for sustained elevation or more typically downwards to ground.

The penultimate stroke sets up the intention for the final stroke. The next to last stroke of the mallet typically mirrors the ultimate stroke. It is usually played as a polarity, a contrast, and a natural lead-in that yields an expected completion. The two final strokes are a pair, almost like a rhyming couplet, that brings union to the duality of the two sounds. This could be something as simple as an upstroke above the center of the gong and then a final down stroke below the center. Regardless, the penultimate stroke must lead naturally and expectedly to the final stroke. The final sound of a gong session is the blending of these two strokes into a satisfying sense of being in oneness and not in conflict.

A simple closing sequence is to play the gong with an "Up 0" strike followed with a closing and longer "Down 0" strike. In general, a down stroke on the gong is heard as a closing sound while an up stroke is an opening sound.

The sound of the last stroke is often allowed to naturally decay though the final cycle of returning sound waves. A natural decay of the last stroke extends the space and keeps the listener suspended in their processing. After the last stroke, the gong may be muffled by holding the mallet to the center to seal the energy and re-center the mind.

In any case, total silence should follow the last sound. This moment of silence is essential for the listener to fully experience the gong. This is the time when meditation is done well. This is the place where form and formless merge.

Breaking the silence too soon at the end disrupts this integration process, while extending the silence too long dissipates the accumulated energy of the gong session. You will begin to intuitively know when silence should end through a spoken word or other appropriate sound.

The first sounds after a gong session will be experienced as profound and penetrating. Passing traffic noise, laughter outside the room, birdsongs nearby, or even the dulcet tones of a listener still snoring, will be experienced as something completely new. Take advantage of this scared space at the end of your gong playing to express gratitude for all that has come before.

Practice Session #9: Playing a Session of Sequences

This session begins by establishing a rhythm of steady downward strikes on the 9 percussion point.

After several repetitions of the establishing rhythm, the first sequence begins with an upward strike above the center of the gong at the Up 0 point and then followed by three upward strikes back at percussion point 9. This 4-stroke sequence of 3 strikes at percussion point 9 and then 1 strike at percussion point Up 0 continues and begins to intensify in strength and rhythm until there is a "tieing" of the third strike at point 9 with the fourth strike at Up 0. This 4-stroke sequence continues for about 12 to 15 repetitions or about 1 to 2 minutes.

The second sequence is a standard one you have practiced before: the rotation of strokes around the face of the gong on percussion points 9, 6, 3, and 12. The last time you strike Up 0 in the previous sequence, use it as a segue to strike 9 again and then move around the face over the four points of 9, 6, 3, and 12 and repeat this sequence for 2 to 3 minutes.

Maintaining the same rhythm, move into the third sequence of striking Up 0 and Down 0, one beat per point and continue for as long as you played the last sequence.

With the fourth sequence, the rhythm increases as you simply play the Down 0 point over and over again to build the energy. This sequence lasts about half as long as the previous third sequence.

Now smoothly break out of this sequence and repeat the second sequence of rotating the strikes around percussion points 9, 6, 3, and 12. This time the rhythm is a little faster than the last time you played this sequence and it is played for as long as the previous sequence. Make your last strike in this sequence end at percussion point 6 and move into the closing fifth sequence.

Continue to strike the mallet repeatedly at percussion point 6 and then slow the rhythm with a steady down beat. Maintain a steady grounding rhythm as you continue to play point 6 for as long as the previous sequence. Finally still the gong by gently holding the mallet to the center.

Here is a short hand notation to play this session:

A) 9-9-9-9 (repeat for 30 seconds to 1 minute)
B) 9-9-9-Up 0 (repeat for 1 minute)
C) 9-6-3-12 (repeat for 2 minutes)
D) Up 0-Down 0 (repeat for 2 minutes)
E) Down 0 (repeat 1 minute, increasing rhythm)
F) 9-6-3-12 (repeat for 1 minute, maintaining rhythm)
G) 6-6-6-6 (repeat for 1 minute, slowing rhythm)
H) Hold mallet to center.

You can continue your session practice by experimenting with putting various sequences together. Notice how some sequences support and enhance the previous sequence while others may dissipate the energy. When in doubt, return to simple proven sequences and build gradually. A good practice is to see how many sequences you can create by staying with the basic playing points of 3, 6, 9, 12 and the two 0 percussion points.

The Build and Release Cycle Sequence

One of the essential gong playing sequences for therapeutic and transformational purposes is the Build and Release cycle.

Simply put, the Build and Release cycle is an intensifying sequence of sound that culminates into a climatic release. The gong is played provocatively to induce a controlled stressor on the listener that provides a focal point to gather residual tension. The inner tension builds as the sound increases in volume and/or rhythm, much like a building ocean wave before it crashes upon the shore. Finally there is a moment of crescendo, perhaps a multitude of thunderbolt strikes, followed by a metered slowing down of tempo and reduction of volume that creates a deep release and relaxation in the listener.

The effect is akin to sonic shiatsu or deep tissue manipulation where pressure is skillfully applied so a rearrangement of energy occurs when the pressure is removed. Another way to understand the Build and Release cycle with the gong is its similarity to Progressive Relaxation techniques in which areas of the body are sequentially tightened and then relaxed to allow the participant to become aware of chronic tension held in the body. The challenging wall of sound in the building part of the cycle causes the listener to "tighten" the energetic areas the gong is affecting and then deeply relaxing and releasing when the sound peaks and the pressure dissolves.

To create a deep relaxed state, three Build and Release cycles are used in a gong session.

Practice Session #10: Build and Release Cycles

Practice using rhythm to build a cycle by playing the 9-6-3-12 percussion point sequence from a slow to faster pace. Build the pace over time to a quick and steady rhythm. Now increase the strength of the strike along with the fast rhythm. After the intensity of sound builds, create a release with thunderbolt strikes to Up 0 and then Down 0 percussion points.

Another simple build and release cycle is to play the 6 percussion point with a steady down stroke for 30 seconds to one minute and then release the sound with a quick upstroke to the 12 percussion point. Repeat this cycle three times, each time quickening the rhythm at the 6 percussion point as well as increasing the strength of the strike at the 12 point. With the final cycle, strike the 12 point three times and then move to a slow down stroke at the Bottom 0 percussion point and fade away with a softer and slower Down 0 striking sequence for 30 seconds.

Remember a build and release cycle can be subtle as well as fast and loud. The distinguishing characteristic is that the building cycle engages and locks the mind in a hypnotic pattern that is shattered by the release strike. Consequently, a building cycle could be soft and slow as long as it pulls the listener deeper and deeper into a sound that locks the energy before it is released.

Playing with Multiple Mallets and Gongs

While the majority of gong playing is done with one hand and one mallet, special sounds can be achieved by using two mallets and both hands. Typically one of the mallets may have a harder or softer head or be larger or smaller than the other mallet so a variation in sound can be produced. Having a second smaller mallet to trade out with a larger mallet can also be helpful when playing a large gong for extended periods. By interchanging strokes with different mallets in both hands, a complex wall of sound can be built very quickly.

Two-Handed Playing: Executing Flams and Rolls

When two mallets are used together, the gong player can also execute what percussionists call a "flam" by striking the gong with both mallets at almost the same instance with first a softer strike (or using a smaller mallet or softer head) that is immediately followed with an almost simultaneous firmer strike (or larger mallet or harder head). A "flam" creates a strong accent and blending of two sound qualities into one.

The two-handed player may also create a gong "roll" by alternating the strikes more quickly than would be possible with a single repeated stroke. This can be useful for intensifying and quickly moving energy with a heightened rate of tempo. When a "roll" is executed, the gong player may find it easier to use two small mallets or even traditional drumsticks.

When playing with two mallets, you may need to position yourself more in front of the gong than to the side.

COMBINATION STROKE: THE FLAM

In this example of a "flam" stroke, the player uses two mallets to strike percussion point 3 and 9 almost simultaneously to create a one beat sound. Note the player usually faces forward into the gong to execute a flam. The direction of the mallet strikes (up or down or both) is at the discretion of the player.

Practice Session #11: Playing with Two Mallets

Facing the gong with two mallets, strike the 9 percussion point with one mallet and then strike the 3 percussion point with the other mallet. First play the points as if they were two separate strikes, 9–3, 9–3, 9–3. Then begin to create a "tie" by striking the two points close together, shortening the space between the two sounds. Finally, strike the two points almost simultaneously with both mallets to create a "flam."

Now play the diagonal percussion points, 2 and 8, in the same way. First play as separate strikes, then as a tie and finally as a flam.

If one mallet is smaller, play it with your dominant hand around the face of the gong on the points 9-6-3-12. After three cycles, strike the larger mallet on the Up 0 and Down 0 percussion points. Repeat 3 to 4 times. Now reverse the hands and mallets and repeat the practice again.

For a "roll," begin rapidly alternating the strikes on the 2 and 10 percussion points with the mallets, one mallet at 2 and the other at 10. After a build of sound, strike with a flam at points 3 and 9.

Remember that the mallets may be used together or you may simply switch from hand to hand during a playing session to bring in the sound of a larger or different mallet strike.

Playing Multiple Gongs and the Gong Concert

The opportunity to play two or more gongs together can open another world of possibility in gong meditation and therapy. The sound envelope of one gong has a natural build and spillover effect as the different overtones sustain and create complex combination tones. When two or more gongs are played, you have exponential opportunities to create complex overtones and combination tones that can be exhilarating. Imagine the richness of overlaying waves of sound that complement, enhance, and synthesize each other so the collective wave of both gongs is greater than a single gong, much like two ocean waves coming together to crash on the shore far above the usual water line.

Playing two or more gongs requires that the player understood the unique voice of each gong in order to create a complementary sound instead of a cacophonic catastrophe. When small gongs are played with large gongs, the smaller gongs often introduce the session or may be used at the end to integrate the energy following an extended playing on the larger gongs. Keep in mind that gongs do affect different areas of the body and chakras, and some may be better played alone.

By correctly positioning two or more gongs, a single gong player can effectively move back and forth the gongs. A smaller gong suspended on a floor stand and positioned under a larger standing gong stand is one way to position two gongs so they are easily accessible. For multiple gongs, players may use an extended square orchestral stand that allows a second horizontal crossbar to support one or more gongs.

Besides the single player approach to multiple gongs, opportunities exist for several players to create a gong concert. When this is done, two or more players position their gongs at different listening apexes so there is a separation of sound as cleanly as possible. If only two gongs are used, then ideally they are far to the left and to the right of the majority of the listeners.

This left-right separation during a gong concert allows for the gongs to be heard more strongly on the left and right side of the head or ears. We know that music predominantly heard by one ear is transferred to the opposite hemisphere of the brain. Thus the gong on the right side of the listener will affect the left hemisphere of the brain and the gong to the left of the listener will affect the right hemisphere of the brain. This diurnal aspect of the brain is well recognized and also affected with through the practice of alternate nostril breathing. Breathing through the right nostril activating the left hemisphere and vice versa. So the sound entering one ear in a gong concert from the left may have a different effect on the consciousness than the sound that comes from the right.

The other interesting aspect of playing two or more gongs together is the production of non-harmonic partial tones. All other musical instruments, such as string and wind, produce tones whose partials stand in a harmonic or near harmonic relationship. For example, it is the partial harmonic tones that allow a listener to group the complex sounds of an orchestra together into "harmonicity listening," thereby hearing the collective rather than the individual sounds. With the production of non-harmonic partial tones from two or more gongs, however, the listener can no longer group the sounds through harmonicity. Each gong will always exist as a separate sound entity in the listener's mind.

This is the reason gongs are best played alone or only with each other. With the exception of bells and perhaps metal bowls, the non-harmonic partial tones created by the gong cannot mix smoothly with other musical sounds or instruments. The best way to hear gongs played in a group musical setting is the gamelan orchestra which is composed almost entirely of gong-related instruments. The unique sound of the gong make it an instrument apart from all others. Gongs simply do not play well with others.

Intuitive Playing

As mentioned earlier, almost all gong playing beyond the beginning stage is improvised or intuitive. As the gong player advances in proficiency, there is an increasing comfort and skill in allowing the gong to play itself. Learning to improvise on the gong is best accomplished by working with proven sequences and then allowing them to lead into each other naturally.

For example, the standard "around the clock" sequence in which the four major percussion points on the gongs surface (9, 6, 3, and 12) are played in a circle create a pattern that can be integrated or returned to naturally as the playing becomes more intuitive. You might find that a steady downbeat on the gong is an effective way to transition into a louder sequence or that the up and down strokes above and below the center of the gong create a centering effect from which to make a transition into another sequence.

By adopting a number of these standard stroke sequences, you can use them as bridges or foundations for your improvisation. An effective way to practice is to do a yoga practice or meditation before you play the gong. In this neutral meditative state, without any attention to pleasing yourself or an audience, be spontaneous and drop the desire to be clever or be in control. Listen to where the gong asks you to strike next. Do not be attached to a particular sound you create. Realize that a gong experience is always unique, irreproducible by yourself or others, and lives in the moment it is delivered.

The Unstruck Sound: Anahata Nada

Another aspect of intuitive playing is allowing silence to be part of the sound. A powerful concept in Nada Yoga (the Yoga of Sound) is Anahata–the unstruck sound, the sound beyond the physical sound. It is the Anahata, the unheard sound, the yogi meditates upon in the final stages of Nada Yoga. This internal sound does not come from the material world but may be experienced through its manifestation, just as the unstruck sound of the gong is experienced through the struck sound.

This play between Ahata Nada, the heard sound that is experienced on the sensual level from the vibration traveling through the air, and the Anahata Nada, the cosmic unheard sound experienced in the silence of the meditative mind through the subtle vibrations of prana, is absolutely critical for the gong player to master. It is in the understanding of Anahata Nada that we fully deliver the message of the gong as it is meant to be played. Here is where the intuitive ability of the gong player is tested.

At its most simplistic level, Anahata Nada begins with silence. Silence is the source of all sound and all sound must return to silence. In all scriptures, there is the dictum that from formless silence comes manifestation of the form through sound, or the word. When sound dissolves back into silence, the form becomes formless until it is manifested again. This understanding of the relationship between sound and silence was expressed in the Maitri Upanishad (6,22), which states: "There are two ways of knowing reality: one is through sound and the other is through silence. It is through sound that we arrive at silence."

For the gong player, this understanding of the ever-returning relationship between sound (Anhata) and silence (Anahata) is critically important from both a musical and yogic perspective.

The great Austrian classical pianist Arthur Schnabel when praised for his musical ability simply replied: "The notes I handle no better than many pianists. But the pauses between the notes—ah, that is where the art resides!"

The pause between the notes, the space between the sounds, is where we also hear the true power of the gong, the Anahata. This space between sounds is known as "sandhya" in Indian music. Sandhya is also translated as the space between times, such as the cosmic eons called Yugas or the twilight between day and night. Spiritual practices associated with these "spaces" of the day, at dawn, midday and sunset, are also called Sandhya. The word literally comes from "san" meaning "well" and "dhya" (from dhyana) meaning "meditation." So Sandhya is meditation done well.

With the gong, meditation done well happens when sandhya is mastered in the art of playing. This is one of the final secrets the gong player discovers: the transformational power of the gong comes not from its sound but from its silence. This is done intuitively; it cannot be taught.

Practically speaking, however, the gong player must simply know when not to strike the gong in order to create the space for Anhat and Anahata to occur. The strike, the sound, moves the listeners out and away while the pause, the silence, pulls and returns them to the center. With the gong this appropriate spacing allows for the swelling and building of the sound to reverberate between the strokes. During a playing session, there can even be a momentary rest in silence before returning to the sound.

While using the spaces between the sounds is important in creating a transformational state, it is at the end of the gong session that the unstruck sound is most important. After the last sound fades into silence, continue to maintain silence for at least as long as the elapsed time between the last stroke and the final perceptible sound. The gong player is indeed fortunate for both the sound and silence of the gong awakens intuition and guides the practitioner.

Ultimately intuitive playing is developed through the player's own relationship with meditation and yoga. To master the gong, the instrument of the Yogi, you must first master yoga.

Practice Session #12: Playing from Intuition

Before playing the gong, take the time for a preliminary yoga practice of your choosing and end by sitting in a meditative posture. Begin by practicing alternate nostril breathing without retention of the breath. Use the fingers to block and unblock the nostrils as you inhale left, exhale right, inhale right, exhale left and continue. Focus the closed eyes at the third eye point above the eyebrows as you visualize the breath moving down from the apex of the brow point to the left or right nostril on the exhale and moving back from the left or right nostril on the inhale up to the brow point. Continue to triangulate your breath in this manner for 5 to 10 minutes.

Now inhale and exhale through both nostrils. Place the left palm over the heart center and bring the right hand in front of the shoulder, elbow bent, arm up and plam facing out as if taking a pledge. Touch the right index finger and thumb tip together. With left hand on the heart and the right hand facing out, inhale fully and retain the breath as long as is completely comfortable. Then exhale fully and suspend the breath out as long as is completely comfortable. Continue with this cycle of breath retention and suspension at the heart center to create a space of total neutrality. After 3 to 11 minutes, inhale and exhale deeply three times and relax the hands and breath.

Now approach the gong without any agenda or preconception about playing. Close your eyes and begin to let the mallet strike the different areas of the gong in a sequence and rhythm that is not so much created as revealed. Without judgment begin to play with no thought of accomplishment but only of service. Play from your most neutral and intuitive space and enjoy the sound of the gong.

Selection and Care of the Gong

For the best results in using the gong for yoga, meditation and therapy, consider the size and type best suited for your purposes and budget when selecting your instrument for purchase. Gongs are classified as percussion instruments, so musical instrument retailers who specialize in drums, cymbals, etc. are often your best source for gongs.

You usually will not be able to actually play the gong before you purchase it as most are special ordered from the manufacturer. With a special order, however, you can usually purchase below retail cost. High quality gongs may appear expensive (reflecting the intense individual craftsmanship), but resist the temptation to purchase the cheaper gongs as the sound quality is significantly degraded. Gongs with the turned rims, as opposed to the less expensive flat rim gongs, are the best choice for use in yoga, meditation and therapy. The vast majority of gongs used for this purpose are made by Paiste, a European manufacturer also well-known for its cymbals.

Size of the Gong

Gong size is designated in inches (centimeters) by diameter. Most gongs used for meditation, therapy, or orchestration range from 20 inches (51 cm) to 50 inches (125 cm) in diameter. Larger gongs are commonly available up to 80 inches (200 cm) in diameter. Smaller gongs under 20 inches are "accent" or "tuned gongs" and are used with other gongs or to produce a specific musical effect.

When deciding which size gong to purchase, consider if it will be played primarily in one place or frequently transported. For ease of travel (especially on an airplane), you may wish to limit the size to 30 inches. If you will be playing the gong primarily in one place, then buy the largest size that your budget will allow, provided that the room can contain the sound. Beginners, however, may find it challenging to play the larger (over 36 inches) gongs at first. In general, a larger gong will produce a more full-bodied sound but will also have a more-full bodied price as well.

The gong size is one of the major determinants of its sound and there are distinct differences in gongs that are only 2 inches larger or smaller than a similar one of comparable manufactured quality. Beginning around 38 inches (96 cm), a gong played at the middle range of its volume will produce a large wall of intense sound that can envelope the entire body. Even a gong as small as 22 inches (56 cm), however, can produce a field of sonic pressure that can be felt up to two feet away by the hand.

Types of Gongs

You can purchase either a flat or a bossed gong. These are also referred to respectively as a symphonic gong and a tuned gong.

Flat or symphonic gongs have a harmonic and universal sound structure. All the sounds of the spectrum unite to produce a characteristic fundamental tone and a dynamic volume—a symphony of sounds. The vibrations of the gong flow freely from edge to edge to produce an especially intense overtone. The sound character of symphonic gongs is influenced by the placement of the mallet stroke. By varying the striking points, you can produce various high and low sound mixtures.

Bossed or tuned gongs are tuned to a definite pitch so they can be played with other pitched instruments. Their sound is centered in the boss or raised middle area. The boss or raised dome in the middle acts as a barrier so the reverberations do not flow freely from edge to edge. The fundamental tone is intensified, but at the cost of sound color. When struck in the center, a bossed gong produces a concentrated and strong tone that brings the listener to the "center." Generally ranging in size from 6 to 36 inches, tuned gongs are sometimes combined into sets so different pitches may be produced according to the needs of the orchestra.

In addition, there are accent gongs often used in musical productions. They usually range in size from 7 to 22 inches and produce an aggressive and lively sound.

Beginning players should start with a symphonic gong since it provides the most versatility with its wide sound spectrum. While other types of gongs have their uses in therapeutic settings and may be added later by experienced players, a good symphonic gong is the basic instrument for yoga, meditation and therapy.

Be aware that the flat Chinese-style gongs, while less expensive than the symphonic gongs with turned rims, do not produce the same quality of sound.

Mallets

The sound produced by a gong depends also upon the mallet. Ideally, mallets produced specifically for gongs are the best to use. One expert percussionist has said that using a bass drum beater to strike a gong is as inadequate as beating a drum with a feather. The best gong mallets have a metal core and shaft with wool or felt wrapping around the head to produce superior sonority.

Different size gongs require different weight mallets; the larger the gong, the heavier the mallet. Some gong players use a range of mallets to produce a variety of sounds. For example, a solid wooden mallet is often used to produce a single overtone by striking the outer edge of the gong quickly and evenly. A pair of softer silicon mallets can be used to produce a tremolo over the entire surface of the gong.

Gong mallets have hard or soft heads depending on the wrapping or padding. The sheepskin-covered heads are generally preferred for yoga and meditation playing but the harder felt heads (and even a wooden head) may be used effectively as well. Using different head coverings or using a smaller mallet along with a large mallet can produce an interesting range of sound.

Advanced gong players also experiment with unusual striking materials to achieve special effects (including metal beaters and bare hands), although care must be taken not to damage the surface of the gong. In the beginning, it is best to purchase a mallet specified for your size of gong until you become proficient. For long gong playing sessions, a mallet one or two sizes smaller than the standard recommendation will add versatility and prove refreshing.

Gong Stands

The gong should be suspended from a stable stand with a cord made of gut string so as to minimize the transfer of vibrations to the stand. Ordinary rope tends to dampen the true ringing sound. The gut string should be examined periodically for signs of wear and replaced as needed. Sometimes when it begins to wear around the knot, the gong will squeak as it swings on the stand and the cord should be replaced.

During an extended playing session, the swinging movement of the gong may chew through the knotted gut string at the hole of the gong causing the gong to fall to the floor. For this reason (and also because of occasional instability in a tall standing gong), be sure that listeners maintain a safe distance from the gong in case it does fall. Also, be sure that an upright gong stand when used on wooden or smooth floors is positioned on a mat or somehow anchored so it cannot slide around.

In all the years of playing the gong, I have had two crashes: once when a tall stand was improperly positioned on rubber casters by a well-meaning studio owner so the floor would not be scratched but which caused the legs to walk apart and collapse the legs and another time when a swinging gong chewed through the corded knot and landed inches away from a person in deep relaxation (who smoothly lifted their feet while keeping their eyes closed).

The gong should also be hung so it may swing freely in all directions without touching the stand or the wall behind it.

Gong stands are ideally made of solid iron (as opposed to hollow metal or plastic pipes). Factory produced gong stands are available in several styles:

- Wall Hangers-Best for decorative purposes when the gong is used primarily for signaling and announcing. They are suitable for gongs less than 20 inches in diameter.

- Floor Stands-Best for playing the gong in a seated position. These allow for a 3 to 5 inch "swing" space around the suspended gong. They are suitable for gongs up to 32 inches in diameter.

- Round Stands-Best for playing the gong in a standing position. These allow for a wider "swing" space than floor stands. They are suitable for gongs up to 40 inches in diameter.

- Square Stands-Best for playing the gong in a standing position. These can be adjusted up and down to accommodate the height of the player. They are suitable for gongs up to 50 inches in diameter.

- Vertical Frame Stands-Best for gongs larger than 50 inches in diameter. The gong is suspended from a horizontal bar connected to two vertical triangle frames for maximum support.

- Set Stands-Best for multiple gongs. Similar to a square stand with two or more horizontal bars to allow for several gongs to be suspended near each other. These are suitable for orchestral or therapeutic environments when more than one gong is needed to produce a desired effect.

Cleaning the Gong

The gong should be cleaned periodically to remove dust and dirt that dampen its natural vibrations. Use a non-grainy and non-acidic cleaning agent that is ammonia-free. Ideally, you can use a special cleaning solution made expressly for cymbals by their manufacturers that have surfaces similar to gongs.

Apply the cleaning agent to a colorless and soft cloth. Rub the gong with only slight pressure and in the direction of the shaving (if present). Remove any remaining cleaning fluid with a dry cloth. Remember that aggressive cleaning can change the tone of the gong more permanently than the accumulation of oils or dirt.

Many gongs have a protective wax coating applied at the factory to guard against oxidation and dirt-buildup. After successive cleanings, this wax coat is gradually removed and needs to be replaced. You may also want to use various products on the market that are made for protecting the surfaces of cymbals as well. If not available, try a fluid clear wax for cleaning and protecting wooden surfaces. Again use a soft and colorless cloth and wax the gong lightly in the direction of the shaving.

Some gong players say that the judicious application of natural essential oils (such as lavender, rose or sandalwood) rubbed on the gong surface can improve the energetic quality of the sound and "clear" away the energy of any misuse of the gong by inexperienced players. One of my most enjoyable sensations was sitting close to a playing gong and being enveloped both by perceptible sound waves and wafts of sandalwood aroma as it swung back and forth.

Transporting and Handling the Gong

Even a small chip or dent can adversely affect the natural sound of the gong. A chipped gong is impossible to repair. Gongs can only be re-tuned at the factory. Follow these rules when setting up, handling or transporting a gong:

- Gongs should never be set on their edge. They may fall over and the rim may be damaged.
- Gongs should always be laid face down with the rim side up when transported or stored. Care should be taken to place no pressure of any kind upon the gong. Nothing should be stacked on a gong.
- Gongs should be covered with blanket or rubber foam when transported or stored to protect the surface from scratches and dings.

- Gongs should be hung securely from a stable stand with sufficient swing room away from walls and other objects.
- Gongs should only be struck with proper mallets that are neither too hard nor too sharp. While other materials have been used to strike a gong to produce a special effect (including hands, triangle beater, timpani sticks, and cymbals), appropriate care must be taken to avoid mistuning or damaging the gong.

Special gong carrying cases can be purchased from manufacturers. Smaller gongs (22 inches or less) can be carried in standard cymbal cases. Otherwise, a strong cardboard box or wooden crate can be used to transport the gong.

About the Author

Mehtab Benton is a long-time yoga teacher and teacher trainer. He is the founder of the Yoga Yoga Studios in Austin, Texas where he taught Yoga of Sound classes for 15 years.

Mehtab completed a Kundalini Yoga teacher-training program in 1974 at the Hargobind Ashram in San Rafael, California where he taught Kundalini Yoga in public schools and drug rehabilitation programs. He has trained hundreds of yoga teachers in Kundalini and Hatha traditions and has certified yoga teachers and therapists in the art of playing the gong for meditation and relaxation. He has an educational background in psychology with advanced training in Integrative Yoga Therapy.

Mehtab is the recipient of the International Kundalini Yoga Teachers Association Building Communities in Yoga award and has taught KundaliniYoga to students and teachers from around the world at annual Kundalini Yoga Summer Solstice gathering in New Mexico as well as trainings in Europe, Mexico and Central America. He served on the Board of Directors for the 3HO Foundation, dedicated to spreading teachings of Kundalini Yoga as taught by Yogi Bhajan.

Mehtab is the author of twelve books on yoga, astrology, gardening and health and is a certified Vedic astrologer and the author of the book Astrology Yoga: Cosmic Cycles of Transformation.

Glossary

Ahata-Heard sound.

Anahad-Unheard sound.

Anahata Nada-The unstruck sound, the sound beyond sound.

Anamaya Kosha-Physical body.

Anandamaya Kosha-Bliss body.

Asana-Yoga posture.

Attack-Moment of sound production.

Bij Mantra-Seed or primal mantra.

Boss Gong-Gong with a raised center.

Breath of Fire-Kundalini Yoga pranayama characterized by a rhythmical equal inhale and exhale breath at the rate of 2–3 times per second.

Build and Release Cycle-Gong playing sequence that builds in intensity before subsiding.

Chakra-Energy center in the subtle body.

Combination Strokes-Two or more gong strikes played in association.

Combination Tones-A tone produced from the interaction of several sounds.

Dermatomes-Surface areas of skin extending from the spine throughout the body connected to different organs.

Flam-A double strike on the gong with two mallets almost simulataneously.

Gong Yoga-An integration of the sound of the gong (Nada Yoga) with sequences of asanas, mudras, bandhas, paranayams, mantras, meditation and relaxation.

Gong Yoga Therapy-The use of Gong Yoga and Yoga Nidra to create a receptive body-mind state in which specific healing may occur.

Ida-The primary energy channel on the left side of the subtle body that carries the lunar energy through the chakras.

Idiophones-Musical instruments that make a sound when scrapped, rubbed, or hit without the intervention of other materials and where the sounding substance is its own source of vibration (e.g., a gong).

Koshas-The sheaths of existence.

Kriya-An established sequence of asanas, paranayamas, mudras and meditations to produce a specific effect.

Kundalini Energy-The evolutionary energy of transformation.

Kundalini Yoga-The yoga of awareness characterized by the chakra system and, as taught by Yogi Bhajan, an emphasis on the sound current.

Laya Yoga-The yoga of absorption and merger, often through a sound current.

Manamaya Kosha-The emotional body.

Mantra-Sacred energy encased within a sound structure.

Muffle-Stilling of the gong and dampening of the sound by holding the mallet against its surface.

Nada Yoga-The yoga of sound and music.

Nadis-The energy channels of the subtle body that carry prana.

Penultimate Strike-The next to last strike that ends a gong playing session.

Percussion Point-A specific striking point on the playing area of the gong.

Pingala-The primary energy channel on the right side of the subtle body that carries the solar energy through the chakras.

Prana-Vital life force, universal energy.

Pranamaya Kosha-The pranic or breath body.

Pranayama-The cultivation, conservation and control of prana through yogic techniques, often associated with breath regulation.

Roll-A rapid playing on the surface of the gong with two mallets at the same time.

Samskaras-Usually hidden karmic forces from the past that are behind many of our actions and conditions.

Sandhya-The space between sounds.

Shunya-A zero-pointedness or nothingness, where inner truth can be accessed and visions spontaneously arise.

Slur-Two or more strikes on different percussion points played as a single beat.

Sound Envelope-The sound produced by a musical instrument after the initial attack.

Subtle Body-The energy body composed of the pranamaya kosha, the manamaya kosha and the vijnanamaya kosha.

Sushumna-The central energy channel of the subtle, body along which the chakras reside that carries the Kundalini Energy.

Sweet Spot-The striking area of the gong that produces the most natural and rich sound when struck.

Symphonic Gong-A gong with a turned rim specially tuned to produce a rich wall of sound.

Thunderbolt Strike-A directed forceful strike by the mallet.

Tie-Two or more strikes on the same percussion point played as a single beat.

Ultimate Strike-The final mallet strike of a gong playing session that signals the end.

Vijnanamaya Kosha-The knowledge body.

Yoga Nidra-Yogic sleep, characterized by full awareness while in a profound state of relaxation.

Resources

Trainings and Workshops
The author is available for workshops and trainings in Gong Yoga for certification as a Gong Yoga Practitioner.

Trainings include:

- How To Play the Gong – Basics
- How To Play the Gong – Advanced Techniques
- Teaching Gong Yoga Classes
- Gong Yoga Therapy
- Kundalini Yoga and the Gong
- Gong Concerts and Events

For information, please contact the author:
Mehtab@Bookshelfpress.com

Wholesale Book Orders
Additional copies of this book may be ordered for your yoga studio and trainings through Bookshelf Press.

EBook editions of this book are also available.

Please visit www.bookshelfpress.com

BOOKSHELF PRESS

Bookshelf Press publishes books in yoga, astrology, and health as well as unusual works of imaginative fiction.

For a current list of books, please visit
www.bookshelfpress.com

Astrology Yoga
Cosmic Cycles of Transformation

A New Book by Mehtab

Astrology Yoga is the first comprehensive book on the practice of Yoga using the ancient science of Vedic Astrology, or Jyotish.

Written for yoga practitioners with a limited knowledge of astrology, this new book explains the dynamic and vital relationship that has existed between these two ancient Vedic sciences and how you can use this knowledge to accelerate your transformation by working with your personal planetary energies.

You will learn about your yogic Sun sign and Moon sign, the specific karmic issues in your life, the most appropriate yoga practices for you based on your birth date, and the most beneficial times to do your yoga practices over the day, during the week, and throughout all the cycles of your life.

Written by a life-long practitioner and teacher of Yoga as well as a professional certified Vedic astrologer, Astrology Yoga provides you with a personal roadmap for your journey to enlightenment. Available from Bookshelf Press and all major booksellers.

www.bookshelfpress.com

www.ingramcontent.com/pod-product-compliance
Lightning Source LLC
Chambersburg PA
CBHW030104240426
43661CB00001B/15